"Preachers are to bring alive the word of God such that individuals and the church are transformed by God's grace. Amy Richter and Joe Pagano bring alive the Word by thorough scholarship and vivid imagery, focused on faith experienced in daily living. Through Advent, Christmas, and Epiphany, they witness in their words to the power of God's love as an incarnate—flesh and bone—reality for contemporary Christians."

—JOHN L. RABB
Bishop Suffragan (Ret.), Maryland

Love in Flesh and Bone

Love in Flesh and Bone

Exploring the Christmas Mystery

Joseph S. Pagano
and
Amy E. Richter

Foreword by Stephen E. Fowl

WIPF & STOCK • Eugene, Oregon

LOVE IN FLESH AND BONE
Exploring the Christmas Mystery

Copyright © 2014 Joseph S. Pagano and Amy E. Richter. All rights reserved. Except for brief quotations in critical publications or reviews, no part of this book may be reproduced in any manner without prior written permission from the publisher. Write: Permissions, Wipf and Stock Publishers, 199 W. 8th Ave., Suite 3, Eugene, OR 97401.

Wipf & Stock
An Imprint of Wipf and Stock Publishers
199 W. 8th Ave., Suite 3
Eugene, OR 97401

www.wipfandstock.com

ISBN 13: 978-1-62564-206-6

Manufactured in the U.S.A.

All Scripture quotations, unless otherwise indicated, are taken from the New Revised Standard Version Bible, copyright © 1989 National Council of the Churches of Christ in the United States of America. Used by permission. All rights reserved.

*Dedicated to the people of
St. Anne's Episcopal Church, Annapolis, Maryland*

Contents

Foreword by Stephen E. Fowl

Acknowledgements

Introduction   1

1 Preparing Our Flesh to See God in the Flesh—Sermons for Advent   11

God's Paths
Not the Way It's Supposed to Be
Parking Lots and Preparation
Who's Your Daddy?

2 God With Us—Sermons for Christmas   33

Up All Night
Remember the Future
An Ability to Communicate
Holy Name
The Search

3 A God We Can See, Hear, Taste, and Touch—Sermons for Epiphany   59

Why They're Called Wise
Red Rover, Red Rover, We Call . . .
A Sign from God
Exile and Return
What Love Does and Doesn't

Contents

The Holy
Slow and Steady
Forgive
Resurrection Bodies
Seeing Jesus

Bibliography   121

Foreword

The vocation of the scholar-priest has fallen on hard times in most American denominations. There are many reasons for this. The demands of parish life and the demands of the academy are both so extensive that they force clergy into the role of either a parish priest or an academic. In addition, Christians in churches suspect that academic theology is obscure, abstract, and profoundly disconnected from the life of faith; they don't think clergy should be spending much time with it. Many, but by no means all, academic theologians produce works that sustain those suspicions. For these and other reasons, there are fewer and fewer scholar-priests serving in the church.

Amy Richter and Joe Pagano buck this trend. They are both scholars and priests. They have earned PhDs; they have written scholarly works; they have taught in universities and seminaries. Yet, at their core, they are priests for the church and minister to a lively and exciting parish in the heart of Annapolis, Maryland. Now, as in former times, one of the best ways to bring the rich fruits of the scholarship of such priests to a wider audience is to publish their sermons. Doing so brings to us tidbits from the table at which parishioners at St. Anne's feast on a weekly basis.

Love in Flesh and Bone is their second book of sermons. These sermons cover the seasons beginning with Advent through Epiphany. This combination seems especially apt. Advent begins in darkness and moves toward the dawning light that has come into the world in the birth of Jesus. As we move into Epiphany we are invited to dwell in the shining of that light, absorbing it, being enlightened and transformed by it, as we prepare to journey with Jesus through Lent to the cross.

Foreword

As you read through these sermons, however, you will not be simply brought along a path from the darkness of a broken world into the bright light of salvation. Instead, Joe and Amy invite us to marvel at the particular fact that God brings light and life by taking on human flesh, by being born to poor parents in an obscure corner of the Roman Empire. There is no reason except God's unbreakable love for us that can account for bringing about our salvation through the incarnation of the Son. Hence, *Love in Flesh and Bone*.

The sermons for both Advent 1 and the Last Sunday of Epiphany include stories of climbing (or attempting to climb) mountains. As Advent begins we become aware of the importance of finding our way on the correct path. In these early stages of Advent we learn that God has neither abandoned nor, as Amy says, "left us to wander through our lives aimlessly, or without direction, or without hope of reaching a worthy goal." Nevertheless, the relentless demands of our daily lives threaten to distract us into directionless, aimless, wandering. Slowly, persistently, quietly, Advent invites us to set aside the time required to redirect our attentions, desires, and hopes so that we will be able to see God's love take flesh in a barn in Judea and rejoice with the shepherds in this surprising mystery.

Once the Son of God becomes incarnate, Jesus becomes the object of intense searching. Herod searches for Jesus to kill him; Simeon announces that the newly born Jesus fulfills his lifelong search for God's salvation. Finally, in the reading for Christmas 2, Mary and Joseph search for their lost boy and find him, at last, in the temple, in his Father's house. Joe and Amy describe the essence of this search with great eloquence, saying, "As Christians we know that all our searching finds its meaning through God, especially as revealed to us in Jesus Christ. To paraphrase Thomas Aquinas, we flesh and blood human beings, have a natural desire for a supernatural end. That means happiness for us does not consist of wealth, honor, fame, glory, or pleasure. Happiness is found only in God. As paradoxical as it may sound, our flesh desires God. The great miracle is that God meets that human desire by becoming flesh."

Epiphany offers us light as we step into a new world illuminated by the birth of a child and begin to discern our own path.

Foreword

Whatever the distinct contours of our particular journey, Epiphany calls us to recognize that God has called us to holiness. Indeed, as Lev 19:2 and 1 Pet 1:16 indicate, our goal in Epiphany and always is God's own holiness. As Joe and Amy point out, if we really come to grips with this recognition, it is terrifying. Just as Isaiah is terrified by God's holiness, however, Joe reminds us that terror is just the beginning of our encounter with God's holiness. "God's holiness is righteous, it is an ethical holiness, in whose presence we sense our own creatureliness and sinfulness. But God's holiness is also gracious; it lifts us up, cleanses us with holy fire, and sends us into the world in loyal service to God's salvific purposes."

At its climax Epiphany ends on a mountain where the transfigured Christ prepares himself and his followers for the long journey to Jerusalem and death. Amy and Joe remind us that the glory of the transfiguration, like the glory one encounters upon attaining the summit of a mountain, is not the end point of Jesus' ministry. Rather, as Joe says, "We, like Peter, need to learn this. What Peter failed to understand was that God had work for Jesus to do back down in the valley. Jesus came to meet people not just on mountaintops, but in the pain and toil and humdrum of everyday life. From this point on in the gospel, everything will move toward Jerusalem, toward Jesus' suffering and death and resurrection. And it will not be an easy way. It will be the way of costly service. And Jesus calls his disciples down from the mountaintop to follow him in this way of costly service."

It would be easy to conclude that these are extraordinary sermons. They edify, refresh, and richly repay repeated reading. They are not, however, extraordinary in the sense that they are out of the ordinary, disembodied reflections of rare homiletic genius. Rather, they represent the regular and repeated application of imaginations disciplined by prayer and enlivened by years of scholarly, loving attention to the biblical texts. They are, in their own way, manifestations of love in flesh and bone.

Acknowledgments

We thank our diocesan bishop, the Right Rev. Eugene Taylor Sutton, with whom it is a pleasure to serve. We also thank our colleagues in pastoral ministry in the Diocese of Maryland and beyond who labor day in and day out to bear witness to God's love in the communities they serve.

Thank you to our family, Mary and Stephen Pagano, Steve and Kristen Pagano, Sam and Giada Pagano, Rich Pagano and Christine Mackenzie, Ellie Pagano, and Joe Pagano, George and Pat Richter, June Richter, Andrew Richter and Jeni Prough, Emmet Richter, and Joel Richter and Patrick Gillingham for all their love and support.

Thanks to Elizabeth and Doug Kinney and to Kitty and Tom Stoner for their encouragement and support of our writing projects. Thanks to Steve and Melinda Fowl for their friendship and for Steve's willingness to write the foreword to this book.

We thank the staff of St. Anne's Church, Connie Saeger-Proctor, Cece Hush, Kirsten Hair, Paula Waite, William Bell, Wilbert Lee, Ben Mitchell, Ginny Hustvedt, Ernie Green, Jill Woodward, Laurie Hays, Ken Kimble, David Merrill, Erik Apland, and Carolene Winter.

Thanks also to the vestry and people of St. Anne's Episcopal Church who called us to serve as their priests. Thank you for embracing our call to serve together as priests in your midst. This book is lovingly dedicated to you.

Introduction

"Our website got four thousand hits by noon on Sunday," our church secretary said. "What's going on?"

For the website of our Episcopal church, that was a lot of traffic. We wish that many people were going online every Sunday to get directions to our church, find our service times, or read the sermons they had heard (or missed) earlier that morning.

We knew the real reason for this traffic was the publication in the *New York Times Magazine* of an essay that Amy had written about her experience competing in a physique competition at the Wisconsin State Fair. The editor of the print edition had titled the article, "Heavenly Bodies: a Female Priest Redefines Sunday Best." But the editors of the online version had changed the title to grab attention and bolster web traffic: "The Ripped, Bikini-Clad Reverend."[1]

> I stood by the mailbox, a small soft package nestled in my hand like a kitten. It weighed about as much as an apple. How could something so small hold such a big risk?
>
> As an Episcopal priest, I am usually much more interested in what is going on inside of people than in what shows on the outside. I know that appearances can be misleading or just not nearly as interesting as what isn't readily apparent. But my package had arrived and the garment inside this package would be on the outside of me and would be all about my appearance.

---

1. The essay can be accessed at http://www.nytimes.com/2012/04/22/magazine/the-ripped-bikini-clad-reverend.html. What follows is a fuller version of the essay than what appeared in the *New York Times*.

Not that the concept of an outer garment, a special piece of clothing to signify something about your identity merely through your appearance, is a foreign concept for a priest. When a priest is ordained, a big moment in the liturgy comes when your priestly stole is put on you for the first time. You choose someone to do this for you: to place a long, thin piece of fabric, color-coded to the liturgical feast day, over your shoulders. The stole shows on the outside that something significant has happened to you—inside mainly, if that's where the core of our identity resides. But something has happened in ordination that should be apparent to those who just have outward appearances to go by as well. "Don't wear your clergy collar in public, if you don't intend to be available as a priest," my seminary Liturgics professor told us. And most days, if I have official duties, I put on my black clergy shirt, my white collar, some suit that looks decent with black, and head out of my front door, looking, at least to those who know the dress code, like a priest. Special garments come with the job.

Now here I stood with my little package that contained a specialized garment, wondering what it would signify, what changes and preparation would be necessary for me to wear it in public, and how "priest" and this clothing might go together. I peeled open the paper mailing envelope and pulled the contents out carefully, allowing my new garment to unfold as I drew it out into the light.

I had ordered it weeks before from a website, custom made. The fabric was fire engine red and a sprinkling of rhinestones along the edging caught the light. I had given the designer my projected measurements. Now I had sixteen weeks of training until the physique competition and the time I would stand in front of hundreds of people wearing only this beautiful red bikini.

I would not know many people in the crowd. My husband, some family members, my trainer, and my gym friends would be there to support me. But no one from church would be watching. For one thing, the competition was on a Sunday morning, with the judging taking place at about the same time as our big Sunday service.

Introduction

I had asked for the Sunday off months before, citing an important personal enrichment experience as my reason. But I hadn't told the members of my congregation about the exact nature of the "enrichment experience." It's not that there was anything about the competition that members of my church should be against or offended by. Despite my feelings of modesty about the required outfit, this was not a risqué event by nature. The physique contest, combining elements of strength and grace, was an annual mainstay of the last day of the Wisconsin State Fair. Men and women would perform our poses of "double front biceps," "side tricep," and "back lat spread," in front of a panel of judges, while at the other end of the exhibit hall, judges would stick forks into pie crusts and award ribbons for "best apple pie—crumb top," and "cherry—lattice top." This was a wholesome environment. But still, I didn't want to share widely what I was doing. It would just take too much explanation. What I really wanted to do was stop explaining, talking, listening, rebutting, biting my tongue about being a female priest, yes, with a female body, and just enjoy seeing what I could do with mine.

I am part of a church that decades ago decided the ordination of women was a faithful thing—scripturally sound, morally responsible. Some people left the church over the decision. Some people still tell me they struggle with the idea, or used to. But many women serve as priests, and many parishioners applaud this fact, and many girls as well as boys consider the priesthood.

Somehow, though, despite our belief that both genders can serve the divine and other humans, it seems there's still something remark-worthy, odd, sometimes upsetting or unnerving about a woman publicly identified as a priest, and it has to do with having a woman's body. For instance, a very faithful parishioner told me he thought I was a great priest, but if I got pregnant, it would just be too weird for him to see a pregnant woman at the altar. More than one person has asked, "And what if you decide to breastfeed, what then?" although I don't think they are actually asking a question. Another church-goer told me I was too petite to be a priest. At 5'10", I have never in my life been called "petite." I think he meant "female" or maybe "feminine," but the best he could do was "petite." Merely holding hands with my husband, even when I am not dressed in clerical clothes, has elicited the comment, "Can you do that? I mean, in public?" I have been complimented on my clothing, which is nice, but I have also been asked if I receive directions about what to wear as a woman priest so that my clothing will be appropriate. (From whom I wonder? If fashion advice comes from God with some kind of miraculous credit account, I would definitely take it.) Most comments are given with affection or just out of curiosity, but I have yet to hear of a male colleague being asked about his choice of clothing, if having children would affect his ability to work, or being told he "should be attractive but not too attractive," whatever that means.

So what about when a priest wears a sparkly red bikini? What about if she further complicates the picture by also looking strong—having sizeable biceps or well-defined shoulder muscles? Can "buff" and "holy" go together? How about "ripped" and "reverend"? If the "reverend" is a woman?

I love working out. I'm physically strong. And, while I wasn't inviting the faithful people of my parish to skip church for the State Fair that Sunday, and was relieved for this relative privacy in the midst of a crowd of strangers, when they asked competitors to fill in "occupation" on the entry form, I wasn't about to lie. So, what happens when feminine and muscular and priest all appear in the same person? I was about to find out.

On the day of the competition, I put on the suit. My trainer checked that my straps were secure, and led me through a quick workout to get my blood flowing. I felt good, almost giddy that I was about to spend a Sunday morning in a bathing suit having people judge the results of my training and discipline. The stealthy nature of my mission—to win the title Ms. Wisconsin State Fair with few people knowing I had even entered—added to my sense of adventure.

Judging went quickly. Each contestant performed the mandatory poses as part of a group according to our age, gender, and weight categories. Then each of us was introduced to the crowd as we came on stage to perform our solo routines to music we had chosen. As each person stepped out onto the stage, the emcee announced our name, hometown, age, and—yes—occupation. I can still hear it: "Next we have Amy Richter, from Milwaukee. She is 39 years old, and she works as . . . a priest! Well, Hallelujah!" The applause was loud. I performed my routine perfectly. I couldn't stop smiling.

I came in second place, runner-up to a woman who worked full-time as a personal trainer. Third place went to another personal trainer who was also an amateur wrestler. I wonder if she told people she was beaten by a priest as quickly as I say I beat a wrestling personal trainer. I was awarded a 3-foot high trophy that I carried proudly as I walked through the fairgrounds on my way to my car. The trophy was so big and flashy, children stopped to ask if it was mine and how I won it. "Tell them you got it for reading a lot of books," my husband advised. Noble, but no way.

I wanted to tell them I got it for being the strongest priest in the state, for being a woman who is a priest with a really strong and healthy body. I wanted to tell them I got it for being brave too, but that wasn't really true, since the bravest part was wearing the bikini, and I hadn't been brave enough to tell the people whom to tell would be the biggest risk.

"I got it for being myself," I said.

Responses to this article ran the gamut and included articles and reader comments like, "Women Body Builders: Why the Church Needs More of Them,"[2] "This would get me back to church," and "God Bless America"[3] to "This is what's wrong with the church today," "My congregation doesn't know I'm working on a black belt in judo," and "Why would a priest skip church on a Sunday?"

2. Robb-Dover, "Women Body Builders."
3. In French, in a title given to a report on the essay in *Le Monde*. http://bigbrowser.blog.lemonde.fr/2012/04/23/dieu-benisse-lamerique-comment-porter-le-bikini-lorsquon-est-pretre/.

Love in Flesh and Bone

The range wasn't surprising given Amy's own feelings of ambivalence about letting church members know about her hobby and the expectations of the magazine editors who thought this would be an interesting article to publish. But there was one particular comment that led us to our own pondering of the scandal of the incarnation: "Well, isn't Christianity based on a spirit-flesh dichotomy in which the spirit is exalted over the flesh?"[4] Other reader comments expressed similar concerns. Somehow, for many people the conjunction of priest and body, Christianity and flesh was troubling. We wondered why.

The incarnation is at the heart of our faith, and yet when we think of a heart as being real—flesh, blood, and muscle—we can get a little squeamish. Perhaps it's the particularity of the incarnation that bothers us. We are comfortable saying, "Jesus walked." But what was his gait like? Would we be able to recognize his particular posture from the back? When forensic scientists release a report about what Jesus may have actually looked like,[5] what is our reaction? Are we unsurprised by the beard and dark features, but surprised or gratified that our Lord would probably have stood about 5'1" tall? We may be uneasy with specifics because sometimes the specifics can get in the way of our theology. Do the particulars influence us to the point where we feel that someone who looks like Jesus, whatever we mean by that, is closer to holy than someone who doesn't? Or can we let the particularity of the incarnate reality of Jesus Christ shed light on what God was up to by taking on flesh to dwell among us?

Perhaps it's not the particularity that chafes, but the real messiness of being embodied that troubles us. "Jesus ate with sinners and tax collectors," is fine, but did he gobble his food? Forks weren't invented by Jesus' time. Did he lick his fingers in between bites? Did the smell of fish cling to his hands and beard? Did he have bad breath? We know the shortest verse in the Bible is, "Jesus wept." We may even be moved by this statement. But when he cried, did one glistening tear run down his cheek, or did he sob uncontrollably,

---

4. In the comments section posted online at www.nytimes.com/2012/04/22/magazine/the-ripped-bikini-clad-reverend.html.

5. Fillon, "The Real Face of Jesus."

Introduction

shoulders heaving, tears and mucus flowing, nose and eyes red and swollen? He walked, so he must have sweated. He slept. Did our Savior snore? Does it rankle if we think Jesus faced the same discomforts and things we think of as undignified, things that come with embodiment?

But the implications of this particularity run deeper. Jesus' pouring everything out on our behalf resulted in consequences—actually, complete devastation—for his body. Perhaps we are made uncomfortable by the fact that the incarnation has implications for our existence. This is to say, how are we to understand our bodies?

Are our bodies tools to be used, and if so, to what end? To what lengths are we called to go in using our physical resources in the service of ministry? Is exhaustion okay? Called for? Or is this way of living bad stewardship?

Are our bodies traps—things to be escaped if possible—physical places where this life ends, a barrier, a boundary that provides the final marker before we take up our heavenly life, our *real* life with God?

Are our bodies temples of the Holy Spirit, as St. Paul says in 1 Cor 3:16–17? If so, what are the best conditions for the indwelling of the Spirit? To what lengths should we go if we feel there is renovation work to be done on our particular temple? Are cosmetic redecorations appropriate, or is working on the superficial unwholesome? How do we balance physical and spiritual reconstruction, and how, and why, do we draw lines between the two?

Tool? Trap? Temple? Our lives are known and lived in our bodies. If we experience grace, it is in our bodies. If we experience love, it is in our bodies. Anger is accompanied by a rise in temperature and blood pressure. We clench our fists and grit our teeth, and our anger is *in* these actions, not merely expressed by these involuntary responses. When a baby grasps our finger with her tiny hand we don't think, "Oh, what an interesting natural development of infant reflexes." We think, "Look! She likes me!" And we make funny sounds, "Awwh! Aren't you just the cutest thing ever? Yes you are." And we smile. We feel somehow connected and hopeful for the whole human race, if only for a moment.

We know the joys and the sorrows, the gifts and frustrations that come with being flesh and blood humans. And so we innately understand that it is awesome and wondrous and scandalous that God became incarnate for us.

We also understand that this is very good news. The incarnation means that God is with us no matter what. That God didn't just imbue humanity with the image of God, but chose to become human means that God's love touches us, and can transform us, completely. God touches not just our spirits, or souls or good thoughts or best intentions, but our whole selves—which actually don't seem divisible into body and spirit, no matter how much we may feel or want there to be such a dichotomy. God understands completely, in the way a human understands, with all the particularity, discomfort, joy, and wonder that we feel, what it is to be one of us, and one with us.

The sermons in this book are reflections on the mystery of the incarnation. They are based on biblical texts appointed in the Revised Common Lectionary for the seasons of Advent, Christmas, and Epiphany. These liturgical seasons of the church year are times when the church especially reflects on the incarnation—how it came to be, how it took place, and how it was first manifest to the world.

In Advent we prepare for the time of the coming of the Lord in flesh and blood. We reflect on God's willingness to reach out to us through the incarnation. We do this in part by examining our own flesh and blood experiences that open us up to, or close us off from, welcoming our incarnate Savior. These experiences include things like hiking in the mountains, experiencing the brokenness that is sin, or doing fatherhood well or poorly.

In Christmas we celebrate the Word becoming flesh in the birth of the Christ child. The church claims in the events and texts of the Christmas season, that the infancy of Jesus is not a prelude to good news but is itself the good news. The good news is not just that Jesus would grow up and become an adult who would teach and heal, suffer and die, and be raised for us. The good news is his existence as an inarticulate baby, his being given a name, and

Introduction

even Mary and Joseph's frantic search for the adolescent Jesus who stayed behind in the temple.

Epiphany is the season in which the glory of God is manifested. Flesh and blood human beings engage in tangible experiences: God's glory is expressed in Gentiles who journey from faraway places, in an abundance of fine wine enjoyed at a wedding banquet, in deliverance from bondage, by way of forgiveness, and through the hope of resurrection bodies.

These sermons were preached in a real congregation. Its members are real people who exult and suffer, delight, and experience pain in their bodies; people who wonder, pray about, question, and proclaim the mystery of the incarnation. We hope these sermons will be useful to you in your wonder, prayer, and proclamation as well.

1

Preparing Our Flesh to See God in the Flesh

Sermons for Advent

First Sunday of Advent, Year C—Psalm 25:1–9

> To you, O Lord, I lift up my soul;
> my God, I put my trust in you;
> let me not be humiliated,
> nor let my enemies triumph over me.
> Let none who look to you be put to shame;
> let the treacherous be disappointed in their schemes.
> Show me your ways, O Lord,
> and teach me your paths.
> Lead me in your truth and teach me,
> for you are the God of my salvation;
> in you have I trusted all the day long.
> Remember, O Lord, your compassion and love,
> for they are from everlasting.
> Remember not the sins of my youth and my transgressions;
> remember me according to your love
> and for the sake of your goodness, O Lord.
> Gracious and upright is the Lord;
> therefore he teaches sinners in his way.
> He guides the humble in doing right

and teaches his way to the lowly.
All the paths of the LORD are love and faithfulness
to those who keep his covenant and his testimonies. (NRSV)

God's Paths

   Amy E. Richter

Knowing the path, the right path, is really important.

There is a mountain in Scotland that Joe and I have tried to climb twice. Its name is *An Teallach*, which means "the anvil" or "the forge." Twice we have been pounded on the anvil. The mountain is made of a distinctive red stone that glows when the light is right. It's not a technically difficult climb. It's more of a slog—one foot in front of the other, over and over again, until near the summit, which is reached by traversing a narrow and spiny ridge with steep drop-offs to either side. But when you successfully cross the ridge and reach the summit, you can look out over the Scottish Highlands for miles and out to the sea. Or, so we've been told. We've not yet been to the summit ourselves.

We tried a few years ago. Despite gale force winds, we decided to try. We got near the top, but the winds were so strong they were actually lifting me off my feet and moving me before bumping me back onto solid ground. My sunglasses were ripped from my face. I feared the knot holding my windbreaker tied around my waist wouldn't hold, or worse, that my backpack would become a sail and give the wind even more purchase to send me over the side of the mountain. We gave up on climbing in the fierce wind, and left the summit for another year.

Recently we went back. This time we were joined by Joe's brother Rich. The three of us chose a day with less wind, but there was cloud cover on the peaks of all the mountains in the region. However, the Mountain Weather Information Service forecast predicted that by afternoon the cloud level would rise and leave the peaks clear, including the peak of *An Teallach*. We timed our attempt carefully.

Since much of the way is over rock, not a worn dirt trail, the path is marked by cairns, little piles of rock, placed every so often so you can look ahead and spot the direction of the path. We went up and up and up, on toward the thick white blanket that hid our goal. We got closer and closer, but saw no sign of cloud lift. We paused right beneath the cloud line, checking our watches, and decided to enter the cloud, still hoping it would lift as we ascended.

We climbed up into the cloud and were enveloped in thick, cool, moist white. Our visibility was limited to just twenty feet in front of us. All sense of our altitude vanished. We could only see the reddish rock beneath our feet. It was eerily quiet: no wind, no birds, just our boots crunching in the scree, small bits of gravel scrunching aside as we walked. We reached a plateau, but we had no idea which direction to go to end up firmly on the narrow spiny ridge. We paused again and leaned against a rocky outcropping while Rich checked his compass. We thought we knew which general direction must lead to the summit, but none of us knew the path.

It was about twenty degrees cooler in the cloud, a damp cold. If we became separated by more than a few yards, we would disappear from each other's view. If we got separated, we might not be able to find one another again. It would be too easy to get lost or disoriented, or maybe stumble and fall. The white blanket and silence were unnerving, unsettling, and dangerous. We sat down, huddled close together, and ate the peanut butter sandwiches we had packed. Rich took a picture of Joe and me. We look like we are propped up against a fake background, as if someone cut out all the background scenery. After I started to shiver, we decided to give up for today, turn back, and live to return and try again another year.

Knowing the path is really important.

Show me your ways, O Lord, and teach me your paths.

Welcome to Advent, a time for resetting our course, recommitting ourselves to God's paths, to acknowledging, through the grace of the rhythms of the church year, that we are all on a journey. There are many paths we can take. Some are life-giving and some are not. Some lead to wholeness and faithfulness, and some do not. Some look like paths, but turn out to be dead ends.

But God has not left us to wander through our lives aimlessly, or without direction, or without hope of reaching a worthy goal. God lays paths for us. God will teach us. Listen to the psalmist: "Show me your ways, O Lord, and teach me your paths . . . All the paths of the Lord are love and faithfulness to those who keep his covenant and his testimonies." God will teach us, which is why it is important to do all these Advent actions: listen, watch, wait, pay attention.

In high school I ran the mile on the track team. I remember being at a meet when, in the boy's mile race, one of the runners suddenly found himself way out in front of the rest of the pack. He didn't come to the meet expecting to win the event. He didn't have the fastest times. But there he was, giving it his all and finding himself yards ahead as the runners rounded the track to complete the third of four laps. He had the biggest smile on his face as he crossed the line that marked the end of the lap. And then he stopped, walked off the track, bent over with his hands on his knees, and started to catch his breath. He thought he was done. He thought he had won the race. And then he heard the gun signaling that the runners were now on their last lap. He hadn't been paying attention, so he didn't realize the race wasn't over. He did not pace himself for the full four laps and so took the lead. However, quitting with one lap to go doesn't win the race. At the real end of the race, one of the runners on our team didn't realize he had completed the distance, and so he kept running. He got halfway around an extra lap before the coach got his attention and told him to stop, to save himself for his next race.

Pay attention. Listen for help. God does offer it. But to hear God's help you may have to listen for longer than you thought. You may have another lap to run. You may need to slow down or stop and rest. You may have to learn a deep inner quietness in order to hear. Advent is a training time of sorts for quietness and attention. It is a time to allow ourselves, if we're willing to take the opportunity, to listen deeply for God's teaching and direction.

Show us your ways, O Lord, and teach us your paths.

Preparing Our Flesh to See God in the Flesh

God doesn't just say, "Good luck, see you at the end." God's paths have markers along the way.

On hiking trails there are markers, like those cairns on *An Teallach*, like the markers people post on trees along wooded trails to let us know we're on the right path. They're called *reassurance markers*. Isn't that great? On hiking trails, you don't want a constant reminder that you are on a ready-made path. You don't want to see every tree along the route with a marker. This is a walk in the woods, after all, and not the mall or a parking garage. But you don't want to get lost, either. A well-placed reassurance marker is one placed just at those points where you start to wonder, "Are we still on the path? Is this the right way? Ah, there it is—the marker. This is it."

God's paths come with reassurance markers. Markers, such as Christian community, with friends and fellow pilgrims on the journey, are there to help us listen for God, to help point out signs that we are heading in the right direction, to pray for us as we reach a fork in the road and wonder, "Is this the right way?" Markers, such as commandments and Jesus' teaching to reveal ways that lead to life and wholeness and spiritual well-being. Markers, such as the right person or thing that shows up at just the right time to remind us that God loves us more than we know. Markers that help us even if we wander off of God's path, because God won't abandon us in the woods, or anywhere.

But try to follow God's paths, because God's paths lead somewhere. Knowing where the paths go, where they lead, is important too. Life has meaning. Time has meaning. Here on this first Sunday of Advent we hear this reading from near the end of Luke's Gospel, a glimpse into the end of time as we know it. Jesus will come again—who knows when, and who knows how exactly? But he will come. Time as we experience it now will come to an end. And for those who are faithful, for those who place their trust in God, the day of the Lord's coming will be a time to stand up, lift up our heads and take heart, because our redemption draws near. God's paths lead somewhere: all the way home to God.

We can run our own race and pay no attention to the lap counter or the shouts from the coach. So busy and distracted with our own labors, we won't even know when it's really time to keep going or to get off the track.

Or we can seek God's paths. We can listen and pray and watch for reassurance markers. We can allow God to show us and teach us God's paths. We can trust that all the paths of the Lord are love and faithfulness to those who keep God's covenant and testimonies.

About that mountain I mentioned. Joe and I have a picture of that mountain—a beautiful photograph taken by a Scottish photographer. We hung the picture in our living room because it's really beautiful, and it reminds us of a place we love. For me it's also a reminder that we have more hiking to look forward to. On that mountain—and in our lives—we know where the path leads. Some day we will follow the path all the way to the top. The views will be marvelous.

Second Sunday of Advent, Year B—Mark 1:1–8

> The beginning of the good news of Jesus Christ, the Son of God. As it is written in the prophet Isaiah: "See, I am sending my messenger ahead of you, who will prepare your way; the voice of one crying out in the wilderness 'Prepare the way of the Lord, make his paths straight.'" John the baptizer appeared in the wilderness, proclaiming a baptism of repentance for the forgiveness of sins. And people from the whole Judean countryside and all the people of Jerusalem were going out to him, and were baptized by him in the river Jordan, confessing their sins. Now John was clothed with camel's hair, with a leather belt around his waist, and he ate locusts and wild honey. He proclaimed, "The one who is more powerful than I is coming after me; I am not worthy to stoop down and untie the thong of his sandals. I have baptized you with water; but he will baptize you with the Holy Spirit." (NRSV)

Not the Way It's Supposed to Be

 Joseph S. Pagano

Have you ever thought to yourself, *This is not the way it's supposed to be*?[1]

Maybe it was the latest report of rockets falling in Israel. Maybe it was images of the security fence along the West Bank. Maybe it was a report on dead zones in the Chesapeake Bay. Maybe it was the story of the mother of an aspiring thirteen-year-old cheerleader who hired a hit man to kill the mother of a rival cheerleader. Maybe it was the latest family gathering that ended in shouting. Maybe it was the stupid thing I said when I just should have kept my mouth shut.

This is not the way it's supposed to be.

If you have ever felt this way, then you have a sense of the biblical concept of sin. As you may have noticed, it is complex. Two things are actually going on when you say, "This isn't the way it's supposed to be." First of all, you have a sense that something is not right. We somehow know in our bones that when the innocent get convicted and the bullies get away with wrongdoing it is not fair. But there is also a second thing. In order to say that something isn't right, you also need a vision of the way things are supposed to be. You need to know that the innocent ought to be vindicated and that bullies ought not to get away with their crimes. So sin, in the biblical tradition, is a derivative concept. First, you need some sense of what is right. Only then can you say something is wrong.

In our Scriptures the vision for how things ought to be is called *shalom*. We translate this word as "peace," but it means much more than an absence of warfare or a calm state of mind. Shalom is a rich and varied concept in our Scriptures. It is used to refer to health and well-being. It is used to describe right relationships between people and nations, and, in the social sphere, it is associ-

---

1. The phrase and insights into the nature of sin are taken from Plantinga, *Not the Way It's Supposed to Be*.

ated with righteousness, law, and judgment. And, ultimately, it is a theological concept: God is described not only as the creator and source of peace (Isa 26:12), but also as peace itself: "The Lord is peace" (Judg 6:24)! Shalom, or peace, in the Scriptures means universal flourishing, health, wholeness, soundness, harmony, delight. The prophet Isaiah speaks of a time when crookedness will be made straight, when rough places will be made smooth, when flowers will bloom in the desert, when the wolf shall live with the lamb, and the leopard shall lie down with a kid. This is part of the prophetic vision of peace when all weeping will cease, when the foolish will be made wise, when the wise will be made humble, when humans will beat their swords into ploughshares. All nature will be fruitful and life-giving, the veil that separates the nations will be removed, and all peoples will sit down for a sumptuous feast on God's holy mountain. As Cornelius Plantinga says, shalom is a "rich state of affairs in which natural needs are satisfied and natural gifts fruitfully employed, a state of affairs that inspires joyful wonder as its Creator and Savior opens doors and welcomes the creatures in whom he delights. Shalom, in other words, is the way things ought to be."[2]

Sin, then, as the way things aren't supposed to be, is the violation of shalom. Of course, sin is an affront to God; but it is an affront to God because it breaks God's peace. And what is it that breaks God's peace? Twisting the good things of creation so that they serve unworthy ends. Splitting apart things that belong together. Putting together things that ought to be kept apart. The corruption of personal and social and natural integrity. A moment's reflection or a look at the evening news can easily supply specific examples. *Public servants seeking not the common good but their private interest. The human voice which can be used to sing like angels and speak words of truth and hope used instead to spew lies, vulgarity, and malicious gossip. Domestic violence. People in churches not forgiving one another but rather holding on to grudges and splitting into factions.* This isn't the way it's supposed to be.

Now, all this talk about sin may sound like a bit of a downer. Especially in mid-December. Many of us are getting into the

---

2. Ibid., 10.

Preparing Our Flesh to See God in the Flesh

Christmas spirit. Decorating the tree. Listening to carols. Feeling jolly. We even came to church this morning, for heaven's sake! But on this second Sunday of Advent, instead of the baby Jesus and the heavenly choirs of angels, we get John the Baptist, a rough prophet prowling about in the Judean wilderness, proclaiming a baptism of repentance for the forgiveness of sins. Not exactly *have a holly, jolly Christmas!*

But here's the strange thing. We still refer to John's message as good news. After the gospel lesson is read, the deacon will have the audacity to say, "The gospel of the Lord." That is to say, "the good news of the Lord." How can this be "good news" when it's about John proclaiming a baptism of repentance for the forgiveness of sins? Some of us will say, "no way." An Old Testament prophet wagging his finger at me and calling me a sinner is definitely not good news. Others may be willing to admit the importance of John's message, but only as a prelude to good news, something we must do to get ready for good news of the birth of a savior. We need to go through the hard process of acknowledging and repenting our sins so that we may make ourselves ready for the gift of Christ. It may be necessary, but we still wouldn't call it good news. The doctor who tells me I have to give up fatty foods and start exercising may be telling me a truth I need to hear, but I won't really rejoice and burst into song when I hear it.

And yet there is, I think, a way that John's message of repentance for the forgiveness of sins can actually be seen as good news, or at least part of it, and not as just a necessary, grit-my-teeth-and-get-through-it prelude to good news. Our gospel lesson gives us some help here. The Gospel of Mark opens this way: "The beginning of the good news of Jesus Christ, the Son of God." The very next sentences quote Isaiah's prophecy about a messenger sent to prepare the way and tell of John the Baptist appearing in the wilderness proclaiming a baptism of repentance. Can this be seen as part of "the good news"? I think the answer is *yes*. Since it follows immediately after the opening sentence, which speaks of "the beginning of the good news," the natural sense is that John is part of it. Yes, John's proclamation prepares the way for Jesus and emphasizes repentance, but John's activity is also part of the pivot of the ages, the time when God is acting to rescue God's people. The Scriptures are being fulfilled. The kingdom of God has drawn near. God is acting decisively to save God's people in the life, death, and resurrection of Jesus, and John is part of its unfolding. So after the reading about John the Baptist, the reader will say, "The gospel of the Lord," and we can respond, "Praise to you Lord Christ" not just with a palms-up, raised-eyebrow expression. We can really mean it.

There are also some other reasons why we may understand John the Baptist's message of repentance for the forgiveness of sins as good news. First, if we hear John's message and it rings true, if we have ever said *this is not the way things are supposed to be*, then, in some sense, we must already know God's peace. As we've seen, in the biblical view, sin is a derivative concept. We must have some vision of God's peace to know when it is broken.

Now, I like cats very much, but have you ever tried to point out to a cat the wrongness of its ways? It simply does not compute. Maybe, as my wife likes to say, cats are operating at a much higher level of existence than we can possibly imagine. The purring that greets the wagging of my finger and saying, "No, no, bad kitty" could be the cat's way of saying, "Oh, you poor pathetic man, with your puny ideas of morality. Can't you see that I exist beyond your silly, human ideas of good and evil?" I, however, rather think cats simply cannot understand that hopping up on the dining room table and eating the salmon off the serving plate is wrong.

Alas, we are not cats, which I suppose may not necessarily be greeted as good news by all. But that we humans do have a sense that some things aren't the way they are supposed to be, is, I think, good news because it means that we do have a vision of God's shalom. It has been given to us in our Scriptures, in our religious traditions, and in our reflection on creation. We have been given a vision of the world as created and redeemed by our good and generous God, a world made to be fruitful, abundant, harmonious, life-giving, peaceful, whole, filled with deep and abiding joy. If we hear and respond to John's message about sin, then we must already know something of God's peace. And that I think is good news.

A second way we can see John's message as good news is that if we hear and respond to his call to repentance for the forgiveness of sins, then we must believe that there is something we can do about it. John is not saying, "Things aren't the way they're supposed to be and they never will be. Get used to it." His is not a message of futility in the face of the brokenness of God's creation. Rather, it is a liberating and, I think, ultimately joyful call to realign our individual and collective wills with the purposes of God. We ought not to be naive here. We aren't going to bring about the kingdom of God through our moral earnestness and good works. But surely John's call to repentance means that we can do something to at least better align our hearts and minds to the coming reign of God. Perhaps it may be helpful to remember that John's call to repentance was probably a call to a communal and public confession of sins. It probably wasn't a call for me to whisper into the ear of John the Baptist and say I was sorry for coveting my neighbor boy's little red wagon. This call was more about the repentance of the people as a whole for their failure to remain faithful to the covenant. This prophetic call to repentance must at some level expect that we can become more obedient. We can be people who promote flourishing, seek wholeness, and restore harmony. We can be repairers of the breach. People can stop killing each other. Hungry people can get fed. Parents can love their families and raise healthy children. Enemies can become friends. It is good and indeed joyful news to know that we are free to respond to God's call to shalom.

Finally, we can hear John's message about a baptism of repentance for the forgiveness of sins as good news because if we already know God's peace, if we can respond to the call of God's peace, then in some deep way we must already trust in the eventual triumph of God's peace. In our gospel lesson, John says, "The one who is more powerful than I is coming after me; I am not worthy to stoop down and untie the thong of his sandal. I have baptized you with water; but he will baptize you with the Holy Spirit." I don't think I would have the ability to truly confess my sins if I didn't at some deep level believe in the genuineness of forgiveness. Otherwise, I would seek to evade, distort, and excuse my behavior rather than see it for what it truly is. The fact that I often seek to evade, distort, and excuse myself says more about my lack of faith in God's forgiveness than about my sinful condition. And I don't think I would have the courage to try to align my heart and mind to God's kingdom unless I really believed in its coming. Mark uses a passage from the prophet Isaiah to describe John that says, "A voice cries out: 'In the wilderness prepare the way of the Lord, make straight in the desert a highway for our God. Every valley shall be lifted up, and every mountain and hill be made low; the uneven ground shall become level, and the rough places a plain. Then the glory of the Lord shall be revealed, and all people shall see it together'" (Isa 40:3–5). It is an emphatic message: all flesh will see the salvation of God. And this, I think, is good news that enables us to truly confess our sins and to genuinely amend our lives.

Things are not the way they are supposed to be. We know this in our bones. How this knowledge gets into our bones I'll leave to the philosophers and the theologians and the evolutionary biologists to debate. But it's there. We know injustice when we see it. We knew it as kids when on the playground we cried out, "That's not fair!" And we know it as adults when we decry abuse of the weak and the exoneration of the bullies. This is not just some abstract principle. When we witness the cruelty that humans regularly visit upon each other and the whole creation, it registers in the cringing of flesh and bone. And if it doesn't register, this doesn't mean that our moral sense is illusory. It means we are dealing with persons who are among that small percentage of the population who are sociopaths. To which, we may say again, things are not the way they are supposed to be.

If we have ever uttered these words, if we have ever felt the truth of this statement in our flesh and bone, then, ironically, this is already part of the good news. Yes, things aren't the way they are supposed to be. John prepared the way for the coming of the Lord by proclaiming a baptism of repentance for the forgiveness of sins. This is part of the proclamation of the good news of Jesus Christ according to Mark's Gospel. To hear and respond to this call to repentance means that we already know God's vision of shalom. We really can turn our hearts and minds to God's purposes. And we can trust that someday all things will be put to rights, all tears will be wiped away, all swords will be beat into ploughshares, and all flesh will see the salvation of God. God and God's peace will be triumphant in the end. And we know this because in the birth of Jesus, these eyes of ours have seen the Savior, who is Christ the Lord, and he shall be called "Wonderful, Counselor, The Mighty God, The Everlasting Father, The Prince of Peace." And wonder of wonders, this savior came as a flesh and blood baby.

And that is good news!

Third Sunday of Advent, Year C—Philippians 4:4–7

Rejoice in the Lord always; again I will say, Rejoice. Let your gentleness be known to everyone. The Lord is near. Do not worry about anything, but in everything by prayer and supplication with thanksgiving let your requests be made known to God. And the peace of God, which surpasses all understanding, will guard your hearts and your minds in Christ Jesus. (NRSV)

Luke 3:7–18

John said to the crowds that came out to be baptized by him, "You brood of vipers! Who warned you to flee from the wrath to come? Bear fruits worthy of repentance. Do not begin to say to yourselves, 'We have Abraham as our ancestor;' for I tell you, God is able from these stones to raise up children to Abraham. Even now the axe is lying at the root of the trees; every tree therefore that does not bear good fruit is cut down and thrown into the fire."

And the crowds asked him, "What then should we do?" In reply he said to them, "Whoever has two coats must share with anyone who has none; and whoever has food must do likewise." Even tax-collectors came to be baptized, and they asked him, "Teacher, what should we do?" He said to them, "Collect no more than the amount prescribed for you." Soldiers also asked him, "And we, what should we do?" He said to them, "Do not extort money from anyone by threats or false accusation, and be satisfied with your wages." As the people were filled with expectation, and all were questioning in their hearts concerning John, whether he might be the Messiah, John answered all of them by saying, "I baptize you with water; but one who is more powerful than I is coming; I am not worthy to untie the thong of his sandals. He will baptize you with the Holy Spirit and fire. His winnowing-fork is in his hand, to clear his threshing-floor and to gather the wheat into his granary; but the chaff he will burn with unquenchable fire." So, with many other exhortations, he proclaimed the good news to the people. (NRSV)

Parking Lots and Preparation

 Amy E. Richter

Preacher: As I start the sermon this morning, I just want to welcome you all to St. Anne's Church and say . . .

John the Baptist: You brood of vipers! Who warned you to flee from the wrath to come?

Preacher: Excuse me. That is definitely not what I was going to say. I just wanted to say, how glad we are that you are here this morning. Just your presence with us today is a gift.

John the Baptist: (mocking tone) *Just your presence here this morning is a gift!*

Preacher: If you are new or worshipping with us for the first time, just raise your hand . . .

John the Baptist: All of you—bear fruit worthy of repentance!

Preacher: Okay, enough with the interruptions. John the Baptist, I presume?

John the Baptist: Who else were you expecting during Advent?

Preacher: You're kind of a downer, you know?

John the Baptist: Just doing my job.

Preacher: Which is?

John the Baptist: Helping people prepare for the coming of the Messiah. Get their focus on the main thing—keeping priorities straight, pursuing holiness that shows they're aligned with God.

Preparing Our Flesh to See God in the Flesh

Preacher: Sure, but Jesus, the Messiah came. You know that. You pointed him out and told people to follow him. You're one of the biggest examples of humility in the whole New Testament. There you were, crowds coming to see you from all over, people hanging on your every word. But instead of founding your own movement, you turned it over to Jesus Christ, said he was the one to follow. So what are you doing here this morning?

John the Baptist: Still preaching repentance. Still don't want folks getting too comfortable with things as they are, and missing the point that we're still called to change, to holiness. Sometimes a little "you brood of vipers!" wakes people up, adds a little excitement to a Sunday morning.

Preacher: John, you need to know that not only did your camel hair clothing go out of style, but calling folks "snakes" in church is definitely not what the church-growth gurus suggest these days.

John the Baptist: Oh yeah? What does bring people into church?

Preacher: Well, according to a lot of church-growth experts, it's spacious and modern restrooms; state of the art nurseries for the babies; electronic, video-enhanced signage; ample free parking.

John the Baptist: It's obvious none of that is St. Anne's strong suit. It was a bit of a challenge to find parking this morning.

Preacher: Sorry about that.

John the Baptist: It's okay. Shows how loyal this congregation is. While we're at it, your kneelers are spectacular, but your pew seat cushions—now those show a real commitment to penitence.

Preacher: Okay. But I'm sure you didn't come all this way to congratulate us on our uncomfortable seat cushions. What are you really here for?

John the Baptist: To deliver the Advent message. I prepared the way for the Messiah, the Christ, by preaching repentance. People needed to take out the trash, sweep the house, get rid of all the unholy stuff that would keep them from acknowledging the presence of the Holy One in their midst. And Jesus came.

Preacher: So it worked.

John the Baptist: It worked, but the call to holiness of life and bearing good fruit in your life is still a crucial pursuit. You still need to prepare for the coming of Jesus Christ. You still need to turn and acknowledge sinfulness, because you are still missing the mark. You still hurt one another and fail to live up to the goodness God calls you to. You still need to ready your hearts to receive Jesus Christ, to follow him, to walk in ways of righteousness and peace. Not just saying we believe and trust in God but showing that trust in how you live. And that goes way beyond comfy pew cushions and ample parking.

Preacher: You have suggestions?

John the Baptist: Enough with your wimpy "suggestions"! No—real, practical, can't-fail-to-make-a-difference commands. Share with those in need. Be honest in all your dealings. Don't use your position or status to coerce or force. Don't be greedy.

Preacher: So, basically what you told those people two thousand years ago out by the Jordan River?

John the Baptist: Basically. But here's where it gets better. Now, because Jesus came and lived and died and rose again, you get to live with integrity, pursue holiness, and welcome Jesus Christ into your life in response to what he did, what he taught, how he lived and died. You're not just preparing. You get to follow. You get to live a holy life because that is really living. You get to experience joyful, hopeful, grace-filled, peaceful living. You can have that too.

Preacher: Sounds like you would agree with what Paul said in this morning's reading from Philippians.

John the Baptist: Absolutely. I like Paul. He wasn't a mild-mannered pushover, either. Comfy pew cushions and parking? Hah! He wrote Philippians when he was in prison!

Preparing Our Flesh to See God in the Flesh

Preacher: Yet, it's so joyful. "Rejoice in the Lord always; again I will say, Rejoice . . . The Lord is near. Do not worry about anything, but in everything by prayer and supplication with thanksgiving let your requests be made known to God. And the peace of God, which surpasses all understanding, will guard your hearts and your minds in Christ Jesus."

John the Baptist: Paul went through a lot of hardship: imprisonment, shipwrecks, beatings, poverty, church fights, being misunderstood and slandered. But Paul knew that freedom in Jesus means real freedom, freedom that matters, freedom to do what is right and know the Lord is with you, whatever circumstances you find yourself in. Doesn't matter if you're in jail or prison. Doesn't matter if you feel sorrow, grief, pain, frailty, uncertainty about tomorrow. Rejoice, pray, be thankful.

Preacher: I love how Paul ends that Philippians section too: "Finally, beloved, whatever is true, whatever is honorable, whatever is just, whatever is pure, whatever is pleasing, whatever is commendable, if there is any excellence and if there is anything worthy of praise, think about these things. Keep on doing the things that you have learned and received and heard and seen in me, and the God of peace will be with you." It's a promise. I think that's why the most joy-filled and peace-filled people I know are people who pray and people who serve. We have lots of them at St. Anne's Church. People who give, share, and work hard to make other people's lives better—all those things you mentioned. We will keep working at those things, too, as a parish family: believing, hoping, praying, giving thanks, sharing, living with integrity, keeping our focus on the good news of God's love in Jesus Christ, and living lives of joyful obedience in response to that love.

John the Baptist: Just so long as you remember why you're here in Church Circle. And it's obviously not for the parking.

Preacher: Peace of God, not parking?

John the Baptist: Yes. Service, not signage.

Love in Flesh and Bone

Preacher: Repentance and rejoicing. Presence of Jesus Christ. Here. Now.

John the Baptist: I think you've got it. You may just be ready to welcome Jesus Christ. Time for me to go. I've got some big parking lot churches to visit too.

Preacher: See you next year.

John the Baptist: Count on it.

Fourth Sunday of Advent, Year A—Matthew 1:18–25

> Now the birth of Jesus the Messiah took place in this way. When his mother Mary had been engaged to Joseph, but before they lived together, she was found to be with child from the Holy Spirit. Her husband, Joseph, being a righteous man and unwilling to expose her to public disgrace, planned to dismiss her quietly. But just when he had resolved to do this, an angel of the Lord appeared to him in a dream and said, "Joseph, son of David, do not be afraid to take Mary as your wife, for the child conceived in her is from the Holy Spirit. She will bear a son, and you are to name him Jesus, for he will save his people from their sins." All this took place to fulfill what had been spoken by the Lord through the prophet: "Look, the virgin shall conceive and bear a son, and they shall name him Emmanuel," which means, "God is with us." When Joseph awoke from sleep, he did as the angel of the Lord commanded him; he took her as his wife, but had no marital relations with her until she had borne a son; and he named him Jesus. (NRSV)

Who's Your Daddy?

   Amy E. Richter

We are on the cusp of Christmas Eve. It's almost time for the Christmas story. And when we say, "the Christmas story," we usually mean Luke's version of the Christmas story. You know, the one with the shepherds kneeling at the manger, sheep bleating and illuminated by the heavenly host. The spotlight shines on mother Mary and the baby. In Christmas pageants, Joseph doesn't usually get any speaking lines, unless he gets to ask for a room at the inn, or to inquire, "Please, isn't there somewhere my very pregnant wife can lie down?" But, that's a story for Christmas Eve.

Here on the fourth Sunday of Advent, we also hear the Christmas story, but it's the one told in Matthew's Gospel. Here, in Matthew's version, we hear the Christmas story from the father's point of view.

Well, not the "father" exactly.

Joseph is decidedly not the father of Jesus. And when Joseph hears that the woman to whom he is engaged is pregnant, and he knows that he is not the father, he assumes what any reasonable person would: Mary has been unfaithful. So Joseph, being a righteous man, plans to dissolve in form the engagement commitment that apparently has already been dissolved in fact.

But Joseph soon learns that the disruption of his plans for a nice simple home life of settling down with his bride and their raising a family together is not actually the stuff of soap opera drama. His question of "Who's the father?" is actually part of a much larger divine drama in which he will play a pivotal role, but not the role of father, exactly.

How fitting that Matthew's version of the Christmas story is about the father who isn't one, because reading further into the Gospel shows us that Matthew's got this thing about fathers. This evangelist has very strong opinions about how people who follow the Son of God should regard earthly fathers and the Heavenly One.

It's in Matthew 23:9 that Jesus instructs his disciples, "Call no one your father on earth, for you have one Father—the one in heaven." Starting with Jesus, whose Father really is the one in heaven, Matthew gives those who want to follow Jesus plenty to think about in terms of reorienting their earthly relationships, including those between children and their earthly dads.

Jesus teaches us, his followers, to give our allegiance to God, and that all other loyalties need to fall into their rightful places in light of our relationship with God. That means privileges that were given to fathers in Jesus' day, such as treating children as property in many ways, and authority granted to fathers, such as making decisions that are binding on all members of the household, no longer apply. "Who's in charge around here?" is no longer answered by an automatic nod in dad's direction. The patriarch giving up privilege and authority over others means a radical redefinition of family, which Jesus himself exemplifies.

In Matthew 12, Jesus is told that his mother and brothers are looking for him, and he replies, "Who is my mother, and who are my brothers? . . . Whoever does the will of my Father in heaven is my brother and sister and mother." You'll notice that in Jesus' family configuration here, there are only brothers and sisters and mothers, and these are whoever does the will of the only Father, the one in heaven. Earthly fathers become brothers, giving up their earthly privileges over others, and, just like mothers, and daughters, and sons, also find their meaning and purpose in the will of the one Father in heaven.

As if to emphasize this reconfiguration of family, especially in regard to fathers, Matthew's Gospel shows us a few earthly fathers. And it's not a pretty sight. There are some really bad dads on display.

Let's start with Herod the Great. This earthly dad had some of his own children murdered in order to protect his position as king. And when he hears that some visiting magi have identified a Galilean peasant's baby as a potential rival, Herod orders the slaughter of the children of an entire village.

One of Herod's surviving sons, called Herod Antipas, is another bad earthly father. During a night of revelry that includes watching his step-daughter dance, he makes an oath that she can have anything she wants, even half of his kingdom. Children need appropriate boundaries, as any psychologist will tell you, but Herod just can't say no. When his darling child asks for the head of John the Baptist on a platter, he can't bring himself to disappoint her. In Matthew 7, Jesus had asked, "Who among you, if your child asks for bread, would give a stone?" Well, Herod, bad dad that he is, will give his child not bread, not even a stone, but a gruesome and tragic dish instead.

But even when Matthew isn't showing us truly horrible earthly fathers, he still pushes us on what our relationship with one another should be, including our relationships with our earthly dads. For example, early in Jesus' ministry, Jesus calls James and John, the sons of Zebedee, to follow him. They do, and they leave Papa Zebedee standing alone in his fishing boat wondering who is going to help him haul in the nets, let alone take over the family business someday.

We get a hint at what Jesus means about the workings of a new family with one heavenly Father by watching James and John throughout Matthew's Gospel. When they are acting like followers of Jesus, that is, as true sons of Jesus' one heavenly Father, they are called "brothers." They are "James and his brother John," or "the two brothers." But, when they are acting like they've never heard a word Jesus has been saying, like they do one day when they try to get Jesus to guarantee them the best seats in the kingdom, top posts in the new government they are sure Jesus is forming, or when they fall asleep when Jesus is praying in Gethsemane, they're not "brothers." They're "Sons of Zebedee."

Jesus knows it's hard to break our familiar patterns. It's too easy to put the desires and demands of our blood relatives ahead of our loyalty to our one heavenly Father, to Jesus, and to the new family of those who do the will of God.

But Matthew gives us good examples of earthly parents too. When he shows us earthly parents doing right by their children, they are bringing them to Jesus. They ask for their children to be healed. They let Jesus bless them. When parents care for their children by putting them into Jesus' care, they act as sons and daughters of the Father in heaven. When any of us cares for the least, the lost, the vulnerable, the weak, the little ones in our midst, we act as sons and daughters of our one Father, and brothers and sisters of Jesus.

In Matthew's Christmas story, the spotlight shines on Joseph, who shows the baby Jesus the kind of care that is in line with what the baby's real Father, and ours, desires. Joseph shows the kind of care that all of us are to show to those who are most vulnerable in society. Joseph follows the command of God. Joseph swallows hard and knows that he and Mary don't look proper to the neighbors. Joseph treats with love and respect someone others would call unrighteous. Joseph acts decisively when the child's safety is at risk and gives up his own home and livelihood to move his young family to Egypt. Joseph acts in such a way that Jesus will grow up knowing his first allegiance is to God, and that means his family will be bigger, broader, and, yes, stranger than any family Joseph could provide. Joseph is not Jesus' earthly father to be sure, but he shows precisely the sort of love our heavenly father wants us all to show.

2

God With Us

Sermons for Christmas

CHRISTMAS EVE AND CHRISTMAS DAY, YEARS A, B, AND C—
LUKE 2:1–20

> In those days a decree went out from Emperor Augustus that all the world should be registered. This was the first registration and was taken while Quirinius was governor of Syria. All went to their own towns to be registered. Joseph also went from the town of Nazareth in Galilee to Judea, to the city of David called Bethlehem, because he was descended from the house and family of David. He went to be registered with Mary, to whom he was engaged and who was expecting a child. While they were there, the time came for her to deliver her child. And she gave birth to her firstborn son and wrapped him in bands of cloth, and laid him in a manger, because there was no place for them in the inn.
> In that region there were shepherds living in the fields, keeping watch over their flock by night. Then an angel of the Lord stood before them, and the glory of the Lord shone around them, and they were terrified. But the angel said to them, "Do not be afraid; for see—I am bringing you good news of great joy for all the people: to you is born this day in the city of David a Savior, who is the Messiah, the Lord. This will be a sign for you: you will find a child wrapped in bands of cloth and lying in a manger." And suddenly there was with the angel a multitude of the heavenly host, praising God and saying, "Glory to God in the highest heaven, and on earth peace among those whom he favors!"

Love in Flesh and Bone

> When the angels had left them and gone into heaven, the shepherds said to one another, "Let us go now to Bethlehem and see this thing that has taken place, which the Lord has made known to us." So they went with haste and found Mary and Joseph, and the child lying in the manger. When they saw this, they made known what had been told them about this child; and all who heard it were amazed at what the shepherds told them. But Mary treasured all these words and pondered them in her heart. The shepherds returned, glorifying and praising God for all they had heard and seen, as it had been told them. (NRSV)

Up All Night

 Amy E. Richter

Who can sleep on a night like this?

We know there are children who will have a hard time falling asleep tonight because of their excitement, or who will be up at the crack of dawn, tip-toeing into their parents' rooms, "Is it time to get up yet? Is it time? Wake up! Wake up!"

There are parents here who may want to sleep, yearn for sleep, be dying for a good night's sleep, but who will go home to presents yet unwrapped or unassembled, a long night's work ahead, sleep a while off.

Studies suggest that one of the reasons the days leading to Christmas are so stressful for so many of us is that we don't get enough sleep. Rather than go to bed at our usual times, we fret or we party or we eat things that give us indigestion. Starting with the predawn door buster sales of Black Friday, we've been up too early, stayed up too late, tried to do it all, and sacrificed sleep. If this describes you, then extra thanks for being here on this holy night, spending one more evening out. I hope that here, in this place, you feel that this is time set aside, that here our songs are wrapped in the music of the stars and the singing of the angels, that even our silence is held in the hush of heaven's peace. Here we dare to believe that the veil between this earthly realm and the heavenly is thin indeed. If we can be still enough and attentive enough, and stay awake for just one more evening, we may even feel a breeze from the wings of the angels that are always around us. Perhaps knowing this peace can remind us of the promise of the psalmist: "God grants to his beloved sleep" (Ps 127:2).

Who can sleep on a night like this?

Caesar Augustus could not. Imagine him this night two thousand or so years ago, this one to whom the Roman Senate had given the titles "Savior of the World," "Son of God," "the Bringer of Peace." In his bedchamber, the ruler of the empire reclines under fine Egyptian cotton and luxurious Arabian silks. Musicians play lute and lyre to soothe him into slumber, but he only ever sleeps fitfully. There is always some strategy, some administrative concern, some farther corner of the world to conquer, make use of, or manage, to wake him up at night. His mind is always working on some problem to solve or issue to deal with. With greatness comes great responsibility, does it not? There are so many people to subdue, so much glory to be had and shown. But does he have the citizenry for the stability, let alone growth, of the empire? Does he have enough men to soldier, farm, harvest?

Tonight, sleepless Caesar's thoughts turn to the census he ordered, which is now underway. Count people. Keep track. Good data will help him control and plan. So Augustus ordered the census and people dutifully set out to be registered in their own hometowns.

And God smiled. Joseph would take his pregnant wife Mary to the place God wanted them to be for the birth. Like his eponymous ancestor from the book of Genesis, *that* Joseph, had said to his brothers who had treated him cruelly, "You meant it for evil, but God meant it for good, so have no fear" (Gen 50:20). God uses human plans for God's own purposes.

Caesar's musicians play, but sleep does not come. He waves them away with a flick of his hand. So many people are on the move because of his command, yet he feels like something greater than populations has shifted, something quite beyond his control. He cannot imagine how correct he is.

In Jerusalem, another ruler is wide awake. King Herod rarely sleeps. Always afraid that someone will snatch his throne, Herod can never succumb to a trusting, deep sleep. His is the stress of the middle man—Rome's heavy hand above him, discontented citizens below—always the possibility of disloyalty. Herod is not a planner like Augustus. He is a fearful reactor, and so his most proactive deeds are always violent—strike first before someone discovers his vulnerabilities. He is called "Herod the Great," but he thinks he hears snickering when he turns his back. There is never rest for Herod. No lullaby will help him. He never catches himself singing or humming, even absentmindedly, even when alone.

Herod wishes he could take comfort in his family, but he doesn't trust his wife. He takes no pride in his sons, his heirs. He won't give them the pleasure of thinking well of them because they may want his throne before their time.

Eventually he will have members of family murdered and will even order soldiers to execute innocents—infants—to ensure his domination. It would drive Herod crazy to know that the only place that will remember his name regularly will be the gospel, the story of Jesus. And even readers of this story will have to pause and wonder, "Which Herod was that again?"

Herod throws off the bedcovers, and goes to the window. He splays his hands on the sill and peers out at the night sky. Something is different tonight in the light. Brighter toward Bethlehem, he thinks. Like all petty tyrants, he thinks everything in the universe is about him. He fears that even the stars have conspired against him. Tonight he may be right.

Outside of Bethlehem, shepherds, too, are awake. Shepherds never sleep much at night. They doze a little, but they are always on alert as their job demands. Night is when danger lurks, when invasions and intruders threaten. Shepherds are used to interrupted sleep, to waking at the rustle of a thief's robes, the slap of a bandit's sandal on stone, the panting of the circling wolf, the high-pitched whine of the sheepdog on sudden alert. A shepherd is not hard to rouse.

Tonight the invasion is of a different kind altogether, this intrusion altogether new. Angels appear. The celestial breaks into

God With Us

ordinary, the divine enters into mundane. We expect the Holy to appear at the temple, at the altar, with priest's chant and aroma of incense. Not here, in the commonplace. Not here with sheep's bleat, odor of wool, gruff speech, hard earth. Not here in the midst of the toil of work, and not amongst those excluded from religious community and ritual practice because their everyday work means they cannot perform the duties of the temple. Not here among those who may neither know nor care what they are missing. Not here amongst the nameless ones, whom Caesar is not even bothering to count, who are not sent scurrying to another region because they are not of a house or lineage of anyone important at all.

This divine intrusion into the mundane signals that God will appear among whomever God chooses, to whom God chooses, as God chooses. And it may surprise us when God does.

It is the light the shepherds notice first, bright angelic beams that jolt them from their dozing. Shepherds sit bolt upright, grab their staffs in alarm. But distress turns to wonder as the archangel speaks in words shepherds can hear and comprehend, words to them, for them: for you, for *you*—you, whom others overlook, do not count, do not know—for you is born a savior, Christ the Lord. Go see for yourselves. Go gaze upon the infant redeemer, the Good Shepherd who knows you, who calls you each by name.

The angels cannot keep quiet any longer. Not far from here, in town, the baby is asleep. But now they are out above the fields. They cannot wake him here, so "Glory to God in the highest heaven," they sing. "Peace on earth. Good will to all!"

Who can sleep on a night like this? Heavenly host, shepherds whose cloaks still trail dust, their sheep and sheepdogs all hurry to Bethlehem to see this thing that has come to pass.

Now, we must be quiet. For there is One who sleeps on this night. Hush. The baby slumbers, cradled in Mary's arms while Joseph looks on in relief and wonder. Now the babe is quiet. There had been crying before, the newborn's small but piercing wail that made his mother's heart break and rejoice both to hear it, the cry signaling the first gulp of air, lungs expanding to partake of this realm, here with us, safely delivered and now sharing with all living, breathing beings the exchange of breath in and out, inhale and exhale, receive and give, receive and give, this rhythm of life, this rhythm of prayer built into our very bodies. Breathe, child. Breathe deeply the air that sustains life on this planet, and has since before human life began. But you, child, know. Since the beginning you have known. And now you know within yourself, as God taken on flesh, as God with us, as God now delighting with a body in the details of creation. Breathe.

The baby sleeps, breathing his infant breath so lightly that mother Mary bends low, her face to his tiny one, to make sure he is still breathing, holding her own breath as she checks. The baby Jesus sleeps, eyelids flutter. What wonders does he see as he dreams?

Mary risks a quiet lullaby, *Sleep, my child and peace attend thee, all through the night. Guardian angels God will send thee, all through the night* . . . Mary's eyes, too, now flutter closed.

Joseph smiles at his beloved and her baby, his savior and his ward. Mary cannot keep vigil—too exhausted. But he can. And we can too.

It is good to be here by the manger, awake to watch and pray, to adore the baby, the Savior of the World, Son of God, Prince of Peace. Let him sleep. Surround his mother and his adoptive father with our love as well. It is quiet, and we must be quiet also to hear God's word to us, God's word of love for us, God's clear word of discernment and desire, that comes often in whispers and stillness and calm.

In this quiet, because we have stayed awake, we hear the promise of God on this night: Mary carried Jesus, and we are carried in the heart of God. God bent low upon the earth so that we might attain all the glory of heaven. God, who summoned angels and shepherds to greet his newborn Son, made Jesus to be our Good Shepherd too, who knows us each by name, who loves us and bids we love one another. The baby who sleeps in his mother's arms watches over us with care and love so we can know peace and rest. This is the message for us this night: for you is born a Savior, Christ the Lord. Carry him in your heart, even as he carries and cares for you.

Merry Christmas.

Remember the Future

 Joseph S. Pagano

Merry Christmas!

What a joy it is to gather together on Christmas Day, to celebrate the gift of Christmas, and to remember the birth of our Lord.

But memory, as you may know, is a tricky thing. And not just because, if you are like me, it is getting a bit harder to remember details. Memory is also a tricky thing, I think, because it is not just about our past but also about our future.

Most often, we do think of memory as having to do with the past. We try to remember what happened on a particular day or particular date. We ask each other things like, "Do you remember the big snow we had on Christmas in 1989?" And we say, "Yes I remember. We must have had a foot of snow. I remember waking up and thinking how beautiful everything looked covered in a blanket of white." Our memories are often about the past, and we do try to go back and remember the details of past times and places. However, I think our memories are also about the future. I think, in a certain sense, we also remember our future.

Now, I know at first blush it may sound strange to say that we "remember our future." But think about it for a moment. Think about how we talk about "memories" and "remembering." When we were children, our parents often told us things like, "Remember to brush your teeth before you go to bed." This is advice about remembering something in our future. Think also about giving someone directions to your home. We say things like "Now, remember, turn left at the second traffic light." It does seem like we use our memories for things in the future, for things like washing up before bedtime and for traveling to someone's home.

I think we also use memories about the future in more important ways. At the very end of Matthew's Gospel, the risen Lord tells his disciples: "And remember, I am with you always, even unto the end of the ages." This was a reminder that gave courage and assurance to the disciples as they went out to share the good news of God's love with the whole world. The memory was as much about the future as it was about the past. *Remember in the future, if you are ever feeling worried or down-hearted, I am with you always. Fear not. Take heart. Have hope. Remember, I am with you always.*

I remember the first time my parents dropped me off at college. I was about to start my freshman year and would begin living apart from them for the first time. And the last thing they said to me before leaving was, "Remember that we love you." Now, my parents could have said a lot of things to me at that moment. They could have told me to remember to brush my teeth before going to bed. They could have told me to remember to eat my vegetables. They could have told me to remember to study hard. But instead they chose to say, "Remember that we love you." And, I take it, they were telling me that no matter what happened in the future, no matter how I might do in my future college career, I could always count on their love for me. I think this was the most important gift they gave me to take into the future.

I think the future use of our memories is especially important in our religious lives. I think in faith we are primarily remembering our future.

No doubt, we get nostalgic at Christmas time. We dream of a white Christmas, just like the ones we used to know. We remember what it was like as a child to wake up on Christmas morning and to see all the presents under the tree. We remember the holiday parties and the family meals. We may even remember what it was like going to church on Christmas Eve or Christmas Day.

But when we come together as a Christian community to remember the Christmas story, I think we are primarily interested in remembering our future. I don't think we tell the Christmas story every year in order to somehow capture the exact details of what happened more than two thousand years ago in Bethlehem. What was the temperature on the night when Christ was born? What color were his swaddling cloths? How big was the manger? It would be nice to know these details; I would like to know these things but, even if we did, what would it really do for us? Can you imagine if you went to Christmas services and the main message was: it

God With Us

was forty-two degrees outside on the night Christ was born, they wrapped the baby boy Jesus in blue swaddling cloths, and they laid him in a wooden manger that was four feet by two feet? It's not really the stuff that is going to inspire great feelings. It's not really the stuff that will inspire great hymns. Can you imagine singing "Hark the herald angels sing, at 10:30 p.m., Judean Standard Time, a baby boy named Jesus was born; he weighed eight pounds five ounces; he was wrapped in blue cloth; he was asleep in a wooden feeding trough"? Not really destined to become a holiday classic.

I think we forego the exact details because when we tell the Christmas story we are not primarily interested in remembering the past but in remembering our future. I think when we come to church on Christmas we come to hear a story that will give our lives purpose and meaning. We come to hear a story that gives us hope and courage. We come to hear a story that reminds us about God and God's love for us. When we come together as a Christian community to tell the Christmas story, I think we are saying something like, "Remember how much God loves you."

Our Christmas story begins, "In those days." "In those days a decree went out from Emperor Augustus that all the world should be registered," and Joseph and a pregnant Mary travel south to Judea, to the town of Bethlehem to be registered. We remember that this story took place not "once upon a time," but "in those days." People use the phrase "these days" a lot these days. We say things like, "Can you believe the weather these days?" We say, "People are pretty frightened these days." We say, "People sure could use some good news these days." When we tell the Christmas story that took place "in those days," we remember that our God is a God who is not afraid of history; that God who acted in "those days" can still act in "these days," in these places, in our lives. Ours is a God who, though he dwells in eternity, is willing to enter into time and to be with us. Our Christmas story reminds us that ours is a God who from the beginning has been willing to get his hands dirty by entering into the very stuff of history. We remember the Christmas story to give us hope for our lives and for our future.

Our Christmas story continues with a tired Mary telling her weary husband that it is time. It is time for the birth, but no suitable place can be found. There is no room at the inn, no bed, no water, no door to shut out the cold night air. The Prince of Peace, the King of Salvation, will be born at a most inconvenient time and place. But now is the time for the child to be born. And Mary gives birth to her firstborn son and wraps him in swaddling clothes and lays him in a manger.

We tell this story to remember how much God loves us, not only in the past but also in the present and into the future. We tell this story to remember that God can enter our lives even when we are at our most vulnerable. In the little town of Bethlehem, a poor Galilean woman named Mary gave birth to a son, and laid him in an animal's feeding trough. And it is here, in this manger, in this very human family, in this vulnerable little child, that our Christmas story tells us to look for Emmanuel, for God with us. Here, of all places, our Christmas story tells us to look for the Prince of Peace. And we tell this story to remember that God's love for us is so great that he can meet us anywhere. We are reminded that God can meet us in the most inconvenient of times and places; that God can meet us in the most unlikely of people; that God can meet us when we are at our weakest and most vulnerable. We tell this story to remember how much God loves us.

The novelist and writer Madeleine L'Engle imagines the Christmas story this way. She says, "In my mind's ear I can hear God saying, 'Can I do it? Do I love them that much? Can I leave my galaxies, my solar systems, can I leave the hydrogen clouds and the birthing of stars and the journeyings of comets, can I leave all that I have made, give it all up, and become a tiny, unknowing seed in the belly of a young girl? Do I love them that much? Do I have to do that in order to show them what it is to be human?' Yes! The answer on our part is a grateful Alleluia! Amen! For God so loved the world that He gave his only Son . . ."[1]

Memory is a tricky thing.

It does have to do with the past. But, I think, it also has to do with the future. I think when it comes to Christmas we are primarily remembering our future. I think when it comes to the Christmas story we are most of all remembering that God loves us.

1. L'Engle, *Penguins and Golden Calves*, 127.

God With Us

In the "here and now" of these days, God loves us. In our wanderings far from home, God loves us. At the most inconvenient of times and in the most inconvenient of places, God loves us. In our fears of the unknown, God loves us. In our deepest vulnerability, God loves us. In our hopes for the future, God loves us.

We could all use some good news these days.

Tonight, let us remember the message of the angels, "Fear not: for, behold, I bring you good tidings of great joy, which shall be to all people. For unto you is born this day in the city of David a Savior, which is Christ the Lord."

Merry Christmas to you all.

Remember how much God loves you.

Amen.

First Sunday after Christmas, Years A, B, and C—
John 1:1–18

> In the beginning was the Word, and the Word was with God, and the Word was God. He was in the beginning with God. All things came into being through him, and without him not one thing came into being. What has come into being in him was life, and the life was the light of all people. The light shines in the darkness, and the darkness did not overcome it.
>
> There was a man sent from God, whose name was John. He came as a witness to testify to the light, so that all might believe through him. He himself was not the light, but he came to testify to the light. The true light, which enlightens everyone, was coming into the world.
>
> He was in the world, and the world came into being through him; yet the world did not know him. He came to what was his own, and his own people did not accept him. But to all who received him, who believed in his name, he gave power to become children of God, who were born, not of blood or of the will of the flesh or of the will of man, but of God.
>
> And the Word became flesh and lived among us, and we have seen his glory, the glory as of a father's only son, full of grace and truth. (John testified to him and cried out, "This was he of whom I said, 'He who comes after me ranks ahead of me because he was before me.'") From his fullness we have all received, grace upon grace. The law indeed was given through Moses; grace and truth came through Jesus Christ. No one has ever seen

> God. It is God the only Son, who is close to the Father's heart, who has made him known. (NRSV)

An Ability to Communicate

 Joseph S. Pagano and Amy E. Richter

One of our favorite movies is "Cool Hand Luke." Paul Newman plays Luke, a prisoner in a Florida prison camp, who refuses to conform to prison life. In a famous scene, Luke tries to escape, but he is caught and dragged back in shackles and brought to the captain of the prison. In order to make a lesson of him, the captain berates him in front of the other prisoners. When Luke makes a wise remark, the captain lashes out at him and utters the famous line: "What we've got here is a failure to communicate."

What we've got here is a failure to communicate. It's a great line. It's also what makes the stuff of both great comedy and tragedy. Remember the comedy routine by Abbott and Costello called "Who's on First?" Abbott is trying to help Costello out by telling him the names of the players on a mythical baseball team. The lineup is "Who's on first, What's on second, I Don't Know is on third." It's all very funny, and it's all based on a failure to communicate.

It is also the stuff of great tragedy. Remember the end of Romeo and Juliet? Both lovers end up taking their own lives. And why does this happen? You've got it. A failure to communicate. If only Juliet could have texted Romeo, rather than relying on a messenger, to let him know the plan about taking the potion that made her only appear to be dead, then everything would have worked out. But, alas, it was not so, and never was there a story of more woe than this of Juliet and her Romeo. And it was all because there was a failure to communicate.

In our own lives, we know all too well the reality and pain of failing to communicate. One of the leading causes of marriages falling apart is lack of communication. People say, "We just drifted apart. We don't talk anymore. We are leading separate lives." You've

God With Us

all probably heard of "the silent treatment." It's one of the cruelest things human beings can do to each other. Failure to communicate can cause chasms to open up between us or it can intentionally wound others in the cruelest of ways.

In our collective lives we also know the pain of failing to communicate. We've heard people say that a crowded city is paradoxically one of the loneliest places to live. People don't know their next-door neighbors. People don't talk to each other on elevators. The difference between being part of a crowd and part of a community is the ability or the failure to communicate. If you communicate with your neighbor, you belong to a community. If you fail to communicate with your neighbor, you're just part of a crowd, a lonely crowd.

On the other hand, we all know what a blessing it can be when we really communicate with someone. When we really connect with people we say things like, "We had a heart to heart talk." Amy has a favorite communication story from a *Reader's Digest* story she read once. A woman wrote about how she had experienced grace and hospitality while she was traveling in China. She spoke no Chinese and found herself sharing a train sleeping compartment with a Chinese couple who spoke no English. About an hour into the trip, the Chinese man made a call on his cell phone. After he, then his wife, spoke to the person he had called, they passed the phone to the woman who took it and said "Hello." It was the couple's daughter, who spoke perfect English. The daughter then translated for the woman and her parents and they were able to share the experience of travel together. A simple phone call gave an example of Chinese graciousness.

And the ability to communicate.

God knows about the struggle to communicate. Our Bible is the story of God's struggle to get God's message of love across to humanity. God tried over and over again to reach us, but we kept turning deaf ears to God's message of love. We ignored commandments, prophets and sages, invitations, threats, and promises.

What is the opposite of a failure to communicate? Saying exactly the right thing.

Love in Flesh and Bone

The message of Christmas is this: God found a new way to say exactly the right thing. The letter to the Hebrews says, "Long ago, God spoke to our ancestors in many and various ways by the prophets, but in these last days, he has spoken to us by a Son" (Heb 1:1–2). A baby. The Son of God, the Word, co-eternal with God from before all time, became incarnate, took on flesh, real flesh, a baby's flesh. God became one of us, and like us, came into the world as a baby. The one at whose "command all things came to be: the vast expanse of interstellar space, galaxies, suns, the planets, in their courses, and this fragile earth, our island home"[2] became for us an inarticulate infant. In the words of today's psalm, God "sends out his command to the earth, and his word runs very swiftly" (Ps 147:16). At Christmas, God chose to let his Word have to learn to crawl first. The one whose "Let there be light," rang throughout the darkness and set off the spark of creation, became for us a speechless baby, limited to communicating through cooing and crying. The one accustomed to the praise of countless throngs of angels singing their unending hymn, "Holy, holy, holy," surrounded himself with new music: a mother's "Hush, sweet baby, hush," the ah-hing and oohing of shepherds leaning over a manger making baby talk to the baby, cattle lowing, the rustling of straw. God found a whole new way to communicate, a whole new way to say exactly the right thing. The Word took on a whole new language, and it turned out to be—baby talk.

What does a baby say? Actually, not much. Without the power of speech, they are, in fact, rather limited. But they do say two very important things: "Here I am," and, "I need you."

And God, in God's love, as the Word become flesh and dwelling among us as a baby, says this as well: "I am here. I need you."

Shocking, isn't it? The Word becomes flesh, a vulnerable, inarticulate baby. Notice we don't say: someday, the child will grow to become an adult who will walk and talk and love and live and say things and do things that will show us just how much God loves us. All of this is true, of course. But this is not the message. Rather, in these days of the Christmas season, what we celebrate is not just

---

2. Eucharistic Prayer C, Book of Common Prayer, 370.

the potential for communication that a baby has—that someday God will speak through incarnate life. What we celebrate is that this baby, the Word made flesh, was already a completely formed message of love, full of grace and truth toward us. "Here I am. I am with you. I am for you. I am trusting myself to you. I need you."

In Graham Greene's novel *The Heart of the Matter*, the character Scobie describes the incarnation and the amazing risk God took in becoming human in such a vulnerable way, a pattern of openness that would continue throughout Jesus' life and in the sacraments as well. The narrator says, "It seemed to him for a moment cruelly unfair of God to have exposed himself in this way, a man, a wafer of bread, first in the Palestinian villages and now here in the hot port, there, everywhere, allowing man to have his will of Him. Christ had told the rich young man to sell all and follow Him, but that was an easy rational step compared with this that God had taken, to put himself at the mercy of men who hardly knew the meaning of the word. How desperately God must love, he thought with shame."[3]

How desperately God must love. Desperately enough to find a new way to say exactly the right thing, which, even in the cries and coos of an infant, turns out to be: "Here's how much I love you."

HOLY NAME, YEARS A, B, AND C—LUKE 2:15–21

> When the angels had left them and gone into heaven, the shepherds said to one another, "Let us go now to Bethlehem and see this thing that has taken place, which the Lord has made known to us." So they went with haste and found Mary and Joseph and the child lying in the manger. When they saw this, they made known what had been told them about this child; and all who heard it were amazed at what the shepherds told them. But Mary treasured all these words and pondered them in her heart. The shepherds returned, glorifying and praising God for all they had heard and seen, as it had been told them. After eight days had passed, it was time to circumcise the child; and he was called Jesus, the name given by the angel before he was conceived in the womb. (NRSV)

---

3. Greene, *The Heart of the Matter*, 213.

Love in Flesh and Bone

Holy Name

  Joseph S. Pagano

Names can tell us a lot about a person's character and the role he or she plays in a story.

One of the pleasures of reading literature is discovering the meaning of characters' names. Authors often give their characters names to tell us something important about who they are and about what they will do in the story. The great master of giving characters names is Charles Dickens. He gives us the policemen, Sharpeye and Quickear; the family physician, Dr. Pilkens; and the surgeon, Dr. Slasher. The Bigwig Family are the stateliest people in town; Mr. Bounderby is a self-made man and social climber; Abel Magwitch is an able magic witch who can transform a poor boy into a prince; and the Reverend Mechisedech Howler is a preacher of the ranting persuasion.

I suspect one of the things that children like about the Harry Potter stories is the names of the characters.[4] They have fun sounds and their meanings are none too subtle. *Severus* is a Latin word for "severe" or "strict," and Professor Severus Snape is a strict teacher if ever there was one. The malevolent Voldemort's name means "flight of death" in French; and in English, Voldemort with a "V" has many sinister connotations: villain, voracious, vampire, virulent, vice, viper, violent, venal, vituperative, and (as we learned in a recent election) vulture venture capitalist! The headmaster Dumbledore's first name is Albus, which means "white." So we may suppose that he is the leader of those on the side of light, who will fight against the Dark Lord Voldemort.

Today in our church calendar we celebrate the Holy Name of Jesus. In the Gospels, we are told that God is the one who gives Jesus his name. And in giving Jesus his name, God is telling us something

---

4. For reflections on names in Harry Potter, I am indebted to Eagleton, *How to Read Literature*, 168–74.

God With Us

important about Jesus' character and the role he will play in the story of God's love for the world.

Luke tells us that "after eight days had passed, it was time to circumcise the child; and he was called Jesus, the name given by the angel before he was conceived in the womb" (Luke 2:21). It was apparently the custom in Jesus' day to name a male child at the time of circumcision, the act by which he was made a member of the people of God. That Jesus' parents had him circumcised and named on the eighth day after his birth demonstrates their piety and fidelity to the law of Moses. The beginning of the story of Jesus is part of the larger, ongoing story of God's steadfast love for God's people. This is no airy myth of a strange god's descent from heaven, but the story of the fearsome, covenant love of the God of Israel who is taking on flesh and blood. If the mention of the circumcision and naming of Jesus makes us cringe a little, maybe it should.

It is Matthew who tells us the meaning of Jesus' name. An angel of the Lord appears to Joseph in a dream and tells him that Mary will "bear a son, and you will call his name Jesus. For he will save his people from their sins" (Matt 1:21). "Jesus" is the Greek form of the Hebrew name "Yeshua," which probably meant "Yahweh helps." Through an association with the Hebrew root for "save," (*yš'*) we get the popular etymology of Jesus' name: "God saves." But note, in the name of "Jesus" we don't have an allusion to the deity in general, but rather to the particular God of Israel, Yahweh, who is called upon to remember his promises to our ancestors and to save us. It is this God, who takes on flesh and blood, who is named in Jesus' name, and who, in Jesus, will save his people from their sins.

"Yahweh saves." This is a rather audacious name to give a baby. Since many of us know the end of the story, it may seem less so. But we should not overlook what an extraordinary thing the naming of Jesus is. Before his teaching and preaching, before his healings and miracles, before his death and resurrection, Jesus is already identified by God as the one through whom he will save his people. An eight-day-old baby named Jesus. In the naming of a tiny child we already catch a glimpse God's plan to save the world through the gift of a vulnerable human being.

The striking combination of the grandness of Jesus' name and the vulnerability of his tiny body is portrayed in Simeon, a devout old man who was looking for the consolation of Israel. When the baby Jesus was presented in the temple, Simeon takes the child in his arms, and he praises God saying, "Master, now you are dismissing your servant in peace, according to your word, for my eyes have seen your salvation, which you have prepared in the presence of all people, a light for revelation to the Gentiles and for glory to your people Israel" (Luke 2:29–32). A tiny child, still small enough to be held in the arms of an elderly man, elicits this song praising God for the salvation of all peoples. But then a shadow falls as Simeon turns to Mary and tells her, "This child is destined for the falling and rising of many in Israel, and to be a sign that will be opposed so that the inner thoughts of many will be revealed—and a sword will pierce your own soul too" (2:34–35). God's love in flesh and blood, seen in a baby named Jesus, is held in the arms of a dying old man.

It may surprise many of us to learn that we have also been given an audacious name. The catechism in older versions of The Book of Common Prayer used to begin with this question: "What is your Name?" After saying your name, you were then asked, "Who gave you this Name?" The answer: "My Sponsors in Baptism; wherein I was made a member of Christ, the child of God, and an inheritor of the kingdom of heaven."[5] Our names and baptism are linked the way names and circumcision were in Jesus' day. This is how we are made members of the people of God and inheritors of the promises of the covenant. In the case of baptism, however, it is the new covenant in Christ Jesus, by which "we are adopted as God's children, made members of Christ's Body, the Church, and inheritors of the kingdom of God," as we are told in the current Prayer Book.[6]

Our names, given in baptism, tell us something important about our character and the role we are to play in the story of God's love for the world. Who are we? Most fundamentally, most deeply we are beloved children of God, members of Christ, and through him heirs of the promised kingdom. How are we to live? We have

5. *The Book of Common Prayer* (1928), 577.
6. *The Book of Common Prayer* (1979), 858.

God With Us

our roles to play in God's story of salvation by turning away from evil and wrongdoing, by putting our faith and trust in Christ, by believing in the articles of faith, and by keeping God's commandments. Yes, we are vulnerable human beings with ordinary names like Harry and Sally and Sue. But we have also been given names in baptism that identify us as extraordinary participants in the story of God's love for the world. With water, the Word, and the giving of a name, we fallible, flesh and blood humans are given the task of participating in Christ's ongoing reconciliation of the world. No weapons. No superhuman powers. No superior knowledge. Just water, the Word, and the giving of a name.

When the devil assailed Martin Luther, he would say, "I am baptized." I remember this phrase as I am driving to do a house blessing for a family whose son thinks he is possessed by the devil. The family originally asked for someone to perform an exorcism. In our Episcopal Church, such requests get passed on to the bishop who then decides whether and by whom and how the rite is performed. Today, I give thanks for the ministry of bishops! Exorcism is way beyond my pay grade. The family asks if I can at least come and bless their home. I can, and I am on my way with my copy of the *Book of Occasional Services*.

I had met the boy once and I think his problems are more psychiatric than demonic. Besides, I'm not too sure what I think of the devil and demonic possession. I've never experienced these things. The closest I've come is looking into the crazed, bloodshot eyes and dilated pupils of a crack addict. I suppose there is a reason why crack cocaine is called the devil's candy. But, as bad as that is, that is addiction, not demonic possession. What if at this home I find myself staring into the eyes of the devil?

I shiver and need to pull off to the side of the road. I don't think it likely, but what if? I don't know if I am ready. I breathe deeply, and, of all things, I remember Martin Luther. I lean forward so that my forehead touches the steering wheel and I say inwardly, "I am baptized." I breathe again, and this time in my mind I rehearse the catechism: "What is your Name?" "Joseph." "Who gave you this Name?" "My Sponsors in Baptism; wherein I was made a member of Christ, the child of God, and an inheritor of the kingdom of heaven." I sit back in my seat, exhale, and now another name fills my head. This time I say it out loud, "Jesus."

I put the car in first gear and I get back on the road. I can be a bit slow. In Luke, the seventy disciples, who were sent out by Jesus, returned to him rejoicing, "Lord, in your name even the demons submit to us" (10:17). In Jesus' name: Yahweh helps! God saves! In the Acts of the Apostles the name of Jesus conveys the reality and power of his presence in salvation (2:21), healing (3:6), and forgiveness (10:43). In the letter to the Philippians, St. Paul writes, "Therefore, God highly exalted him and gave him the name that is above every name, so that at the name of Jesus every knee should bend, in heaven and on earth and under the earth" (2:5–11). I sing the first verse of "All Hail the Power of Jesus' Name" a few times over as I pull up to the house.

I am welcomed into a tidy, middle class home. We share a cup of coffee in the kitchen and talk about the traffic. We even joke a bit as we wait for their teenage daughter to join us. I think to myself that this seems like a normal, loving family that happens to have a troubled adolescent boy. So what else is new? The daughter comes downstairs holding a necklace in her hand. She asks if I can bless it before we start. I take the necklace, ask God's blessing, and return it to the smiling girl.

We all gather at the entrance of the house for the beginning of the house blessing. I hold up my prayer book and I say the opening invocation loudly enough to be heard throughout the house: in every room, under every bed, in every closet: "Let the mighty power of the Holy God be present in this place to banish from it every unclean spirit, to cleanse it from every residue of evil, and to make it a secure habitation for those who dwell in it; in the Name of Jesus Christ our Lord."

SECOND SUNDAY AFTER CHRISTMAS, YEARS A, B, AND C—LUKE 2:41–52

> Now every year his parents went to Jerusalem for the festival of the Passover. And when he was twelve years old, they went up as usual for

the festival. When the festival was ended and they started to return, the boy Jesus stayed behind in Jerusalem, but his parents did not know it. Assuming that he was in the group of travelers, they went a day's journey. Then they started to look for him among their relatives and friends. When they did not find him, they returned to Jerusalem to search for him. After three days they found him in the temple, sitting among the teachers, listening to them and asking them questions. And all who heard him were amazed at his understanding and his answers. When his parents saw him they were astonished; and his mother said to him, "Child, why have you treated us like this? Look, your father and I have been searching for you in great anxiety." He said to them, "Why were you searching for me? Did you not know that I must be in my Father's house?" But they did not understand what he said to them. Then he went down with them and came to Nazareth, and was obedient to them. His mother treasured all these things in her heart. And Jesus increased in wisdom and in years, and in divine and human favor. (NRSV)

The Search

   Joseph S. Pagano and Amy E. Richter

We can imagine his parents' panic. As Mary and Joseph realize that Jesus is not among the group of pilgrims traveling back to Nazareth from Jerusalem after the Passover festival, the panic hits: "Where is he?" People traveled in large groups, maybe with other family members for protection and companionship as they walked to and from the capital. And if their family was anything like ours, then it is likely that the teenagers collected in their own gaggle to do their own thing. After a long day on the road, Mary probably says to Joseph, "Have you seen Jesus?" And he says, "I'm sure he's with his friends. I'll go find him and tell him supper's ready." But then, no Jesus. No one has seen him all day.

We shouldn't be too hard on Joseph and Mary for inadvertently leaving Jesus behind. They assumed they knew where to find him, and no doubt there were many other details to think of. We know that even very good parents can get distracted before a family trip. Plenty of us have been on family trips where the first turn made is a U-turn to go back for something left behind. So picture Joseph taking care of those things many fathers like to take care of. He packs up the donkey, mindful of the exact time they have to leave to beat the rush hour traffic in Samaria and make the reverse commute out of Jerusalem. He's been watching the weather and decides that if they're going to dodge the showers forming out over the Mediterranean they had better not wait around. So, off they go, probably more than a little distracted. They assume Jesus is somewhere in the crowd. But when they can't find him, their search is on.

As humans, we are searchers. We have the sense that there is always something more for us, out beyond us somewhere. Sometimes we know what it is we're looking for; sometimes we don't know—we just have that feeling that there must be more. If you made a New Year's resolution this year, it's probably part of that search—for better health, better relationships, better use of time or money, better fitting into the clothes in our closets, better attention to our spiritual lives or prayer. Whatever we want to change, it's often because we sense that these changes will get us closer to the life we're searching for, the meaning we're searching for. Our search is on.

As Christians we know that all our searching finds its meaning through God, especially as revealed to us in Jesus Christ. To paraphrase Thomas Aquinas, we flesh and blood human beings have a natural desire for a supernatural end. That means happiness for us does not consist of wealth, honor, fame, glory, or pleasure. Happiness is found only in God. As paradoxical as it may sound, our flesh and blood humanity desires God. The great miracle is that God meets that human desire by becoming flesh. Our search for something meaningful beyond ourselves, and all our smaller attempts to put the details of our lives in order, find their fulfillment through right relationship with God, and knowing God especially through knowing Jesus. As St. Augustine said, "our hearts are restless, until they rest in Thee, O God."[7] And so we too search for Jesus. Our search is on.

---

7. St. Augustine, *Confessions* I.1.

God With Us

Mary and Joseph's search for Jesus takes them back to the temple. There they find Jesus listening to and speaking with the teachers. As the Passover festival drew to a close, the elders in the temple held open forums, and Jesus was probably among the young men who were fascinated with the dialogue, those who asked questions and gave their own responses. And the wise words of Jesus apparently made an impression on his elders.

His mother is not so impressed. "Why have you treated us like this? How could you do such a thing? We've been looking all over for you!"

Jesus answers, "Why were you searching for me? Did you not know that I must be in my Father's house?" As Jesus has been growing up, living with his good Jewish parents who are taking care to bring him up with all the observances of his faith, listening to the teachers, learning the Scriptures, he has begun to have the sense of himself as a child of God, someone for whom God has a plan, a purpose. Jesus' response to his mother shows that he is ready to claim as his priority God's will for him, even if it means he must detach from some things. Jesus knows that his search must start and end in God. His search for meaning will bring him closer and closer to discovering what it is that God will have him do in the world, what his unique mission is, how he can serve others and God.

Jesus calls us to live our lives so that the fullest measure of our potential will be gained, so that we too will claim our identity as children of God for whom God has a plan and a unique purpose. Jesus shows us that the way to do this is to discover our relationship with God and to commit our whole selves to whatever emerges as our mission. Not just with words, but with his life. In this case, the life of an adolescent boy who knows his mother and adoptive father don't understand him. Truly human means truly human. And in our gospel lesson we have our one glimpse about what that was like in Jesus' childhood.

Significantly, this passage does not picture a young Jesus struggling with acne so that we might lead pimple-free lives. Rather, it shows us our human need to realign our loyalties to the will and purposes of our heavenly Father. Like it was for Jesus, living out our lives in relationship with God will demand some wrenching detachments. Living this meaningful life in God will open us to being misunderstood even by those who are closest to us. Living this meaningful life will require constant prayer and courage.

So our search is on for Jesus, and to follow in his footsteps. Where shall we search?

Our story gives us some clues.

First, how not to look. We shouldn't assume that it's enough that someone else knows where Jesus is. Mary and Joseph make that mistake. They assumed he was around here somewhere and that others knew exactly where he was, and when they needed him it would be very easy to locate him. What they should have done was talk with him themselves. Yes, our divine Savior is with us all the time. And through the Holy Spirit, Christ is closer to us than our own breath. Always. We are never alone. But, what a difference it makes not to just assume he's near, but actually to know it, to converse, to pray and talk and listen and know through experience, not just assumption and hearsay, that he is near us and around us. Know firsthand that Christ is with you. Let him be with you now, rather than thinking you'll get more specific about your relationship with him later. Let him go with you when you go through the anxieties and the troubles and the searches you will have in life, rather than anxiously searching for him later.

What about how to search, and where to search? There are some places Jesus has guaranteed we will find him. Hint: he says, "I must be in my Father's house." Christ will be with God's people in worship, in prayer, and in the sacraments. In the Word proclaimed and heard. In the body and blood of Christ given and received. In the midst of two or three or more gathered together in his name, singing slightly out of tune, eating Danish, drinking coffee, worrying about their children.

But when Jesus says, "I must be in my Father's house," there's another possible way to translate his words, and this too is a hint for where to search for Jesus. His words also mean, "involved in my Father's business," or in other words, "in the things of my Father." Search for Jesus where the business of his Father is being done. Where the hungry are fed and the thirsty are given something to drink. Where the stranger is welcomed and the naked are clothed.

Where the sick are cared for and prisoners are visited. Search for Jesus there and you will find him.

Your search will be rewarded. Jesus himself said, "Ask and it will be given you; search, and you will find; knock and the door will be opened for you" (Luke 11:9). He can make that promise because he is the Son of God, the God who has been searching for us and longing for us to search for God since the beginning of time. Listen to this promise from Jeremiah: "I know the plans I have in mind for you—it is the Lord who speaks—plans for peace, not disaster, reserving a future full of hope for you. When you seek me you shall find me, when you seek me with all your heart" (Jer 29:11, 13).

The search is on. May your searching lead you to Christ, and in Christ may all your searching be blessed.

Amen.

3

A God We Can See, Hear, Taste, and Touch

Sermons for Epiphany

THE EPIPHANY, YEARS A, B, AND C—MATTHEW 2:1–12

> In the time of King Herod, after Jesus was born in Bethlehem of Judea, wise men from the East came to Jerusalem, asking, "Where is the child who has been born king of the Jews? For we observed his star at its rising, and have come to pay him homage." When King Herod heard this, he was frightened, and all Jerusalem with him; and calling together all the chief priests and scribes of the people, he inquired of them where the Messiah was to be born. They told him, "In Bethlehem of Judea; for so it has been written by the prophet:
>
>> 'And you, Bethlehem, in the land of Judah,
>> are by no means least among the rulers of Judah;
>> for from you shall come a ruler
>> who is to shepherd my people Israel.'"
>
> Then Herod secretly called for the wise men and learned from them the exact time when the star had appeared. Then he sent them to Bethlehem, saying, "Go and search diligently for the child; and when you have found him, bring me word so that I may also go and pay him homage." When they had heard the king, they set out; and there, ahead of them, went the star that they had seen at its rising, until it stopped

over the place where the child was. When they saw that the star had stopped, they were overwhelmed with joy. On entering the house, they saw the child with Mary his mother; and they knelt down and paid him homage. Then, opening their treasure chests, they offered him gifts of gold, frankincense, and myrrh. And having been warned in a dream not to return to Herod, they left for their own country by another road. (NRSV)

Why They're Called Wise

 Amy E. Richter

Forget Mary. No disrespect. I know she's the star, but the role I always wanted to play in the Christmas pageant is one of the three Magi, the wise men. They get the best costumes, the best props, the most drama. The shepherds are scared of the angels and have to be told to go to Bethlehem. The wise men are afraid of no one. They know whom to listen to and whom to ignore. They do what they came to do, and then get off the stage. They even have their own memorable song.

In the church where I grew up, the pageant included the singing of "We Three Kings." The three fortunate children who got to be the wise men, bedecked in costumes made of brocade remnants and scraps of gold lamé, multicolored upholstery samples wound around their heads for turbans, made their way up and down the aisles of our church. Meanwhile I, and the rest of the bathrobe and burlap-clad shepherds, awaited their arrival at the chancel steps to adore the baby doll clutched in Mary's arms. The magi's task was not an easy one, so it was properly reserved for some of the older Sunday school regulars, because their timing had to be right. We had five verses to sing, and our worship space wasn't that large, so it meant keeping a deliberate and slow pace, something that would have actually been difficult for some of us smaller kids to manage.

One year the magi went up the left side aisle, across the front, as the organist let loose all the majesty that our little organ could muster: *Buuuuuh-buh-buh-buh-buh-buh. Buuuuuh-buh-buh-buh-*

A God We Can See, Hear, Taste, and Touch

buh-buh. The organ music created an exotic interlude between the verses. Down the middle aisle the magi trod as we sang: *Fraaaank-incense to offer have I; Iiiiiin-cense owns a Deity nigh . . .* The magi rounded the back row of pews. *Ohhhhhwww, Woah-ohhhhwww! Star of won-der, star of night . . .* Slowly, slowly wound the wise men up the side aisle, till finally we wrapped up the last verse and chorus. The magi knelt before the babe, and . . . "Oh no!" The first magi exclaimed into the hushed and expectant silence, "I forgot my gift!"

Apparently being magi is no easy thing, and this is true not only in pageants. The way of the magi is not an easy path to take.

Even knowing who the magi are isn't easy. Contrary to the hymn, composed originally for a seminary's Christmas pageant,[1] in Matthew's Gospel they aren't kings. And Matthew doesn't tell us how many there are. But the song "We Three Kings" does uphold some long-held traditions about these mysterious worshippers from the east. Matthew calls them "magi," and we will return to that in a moment. But the idea that there were three of them probably comes from the three gifts they remembered to bring. They are called kings starting in the fifth or sixth century.[2] This description fits nicely for Christians as a fulfillment to some passages seen as prophecy in the Old Testament, like this one from the Psalms: "The kings of Sheba and Saba will offer gifts; all kings will do him homage, all nations become his servants" (Ps 72:11) and this from Isaiah: "The nations will come to your light and kings to the brightness of your dawning" (Isa 60:3).

By the sixth century, the magi had been given names and descriptions often seen in artistic representations. One is named Caspar, meaning "treasurer," and he is imagined as a beardless young man. Another is Melchior, which means "king of light," or "king of the city," and he is portrayed as a bearded old man. The third is Balthasar, which means "God protect the king," and he is portrayed as a black man.[3] By the eighth century, the three magi

---

1. Composed by John Henry Hopkins for a Christmas pageant at the General Theological Seminary in 1857. Morgan, *Come Let Us Adore Him*, 81.
2. Luz, *Matthew 1–7*, 111.
3. Ibid., 116.

had come to represent three continents—Asia, Africa, and Europe.[4] In Matthew's Gospel they are "from the east" (Matt 2:1) and they are certainly Gentiles. In later tradition, they come to represent the whole known world, coming to worship Jesus.

Matthew does not call them kings, because there are two kings already in this early episode in Jesus' life: King Herod and King Jesus. These three mysterious magi from the east uphold a longer, more ancient tradition—seekers after truth who sometimes serve as advisors to kings and rulers. As early as about six hundred years before Matthew writes his Gospel, magi are known as a group of religious experts in Persia.[5] Classical sources show magi engaged in making charms, spells, magic, rituals, telling a story of the birth of the gods, and interpreting dreams.[6]

It's the magi's skill as interpreters of dreams that brings some magi before King Nebuchadnezzar in the book of Daniel. The king has had terrible dreams. But, fortunately for him, he has a group of advisors, including magi, whom he can call on in a situation like this. These advisors have all kinds of skills, such as exorcism, magic, soothsaying, astrology, and—fortunately for the distressed king—the ability to interpret dreams.[7] So, Nebuchadnezzar summons his wise men to tell him his dreams and interpret them for him (Dan 2:1–3). "Sure," they say, "tell us your dream and we will tell you the meaning." Nebuchadnezzar, however, made it very difficult for these willing interpreters—he demanded they tell him *both* the dream and its interpretation. They go back and forth on this—*tell us the dream; no you tell me the dream*—and it gets ugly. Finally, Nebuchadnezzar says, "If you do not tell me both the dream and its interpretation, you shall be torn limb from limb, and your houses shall be laid in ruins" (2:5). He promises great rewards if they can do it, but they finally protest, "The thing that the king is asking is too difficult, and no one can reveal it to the king except the gods, whose dwelling is not with mortals" (2:11). The king flies into a rage

4. Ibid., 108.
5. Hull, *Hellenistic Magic*, 126.
6. Richter, *Enoch and the Gospel of Matthew*, 172–79.

7. For more on the wise advisors in the court of Nebuchnezzar in Daniel, see Jeffers, *Magic and Divination*.

A God We Can See, Hear, Taste, and Touch

and orders "all the wise men[8] of Babylon be destroyed" (2:12). And that's where the human hero of the story, Daniel, comes in.

When Nebuchadnezzar had besieged Jerusalem and Judah, and had taken exiles to Babylon, Daniel was among those trained in the literature and language of the Chaldeans (1:4). Daniel was an excellent student, and he had gifts of wisdom and understanding that surpassed even the kingdom's native-born wise men (1:20).

When Daniel finds out that he and all the other wise men in Babylon are going to be executed because of Nebuchadnezzar's stubbornness and nightmares, Daniel requests an audience with the king. God gives Daniel the ability to tell the king his dream and interpret it, which he does, and Nebuchadnezzar is appropriately impressed. He promotes Daniel to head wise man of Babylon (2:48). When Nebuchadnezzar has another puzzling dream later on, he once again calls for Daniel to interpret. Daniel's interpretation reveals that Nebuchadnezzar will lose his kingdom and his standing in society until he learns that it's actually God, the Most High, "who has sovereignty over the kingdom of mortals and gives it to whom he will" (4:25). And so it came true, just as Daniel has said.

Many, many years later, in Matthew's Gospel, the magi traverse from afar, looking for a king. They have followed a star to find the "child who has been born king of the Jews" (Matt 2:2). How did they know, and why did they care about a king born in a faraway land? And why did they care enough to seek him out, to see him firsthand, up close, with their own eyes? Is their searching the fruit of the seeds sown in the book of Daniel? What a wonder—and another example of God's bringing something good out of something bad. The Babylonian exile, all that time in captivity, all that humiliation for those taken far from their homes and their beloved city of Jerusalem and land of Judah had led, in part, to this: The magi, descendants of a class of religious experts, once headed by none other than the foreign-born Daniel, carried down through their lore what Daniel had also known—that the Jews were expecting a child who would be born their king. They knew that this king deserved honor and worship. So they followed the sign that had been given them, a

---

8. Here the word is *sophoi* rather than *magoi*.

heavenly body to tell them about a king born on earth, the star they had seen in the east that led them this far.

The magi apparently had special abilities, like the ability to notice and follow a special star, but they didn't neglect the use of basic common sense. Looking for a king? Go to the king's house. Ask to see the child. "Where is the child who has been born king of the Jews?" they ask when Herod's butler answers the palace door. "We observed his star, and here we are, ready to do him homage."

The problem is, the king in Jerusalem is in fact able to receive guests, but he is not a child, not chronologically anyway. And he isn't expecting any callers from the East, let alone magi who don't seem to know that Herod considers himself alive and well, and that the office of King of the Jews is occupied at the moment. Herod is frightened and ignorant. Like Nebuchadnezzar, Herod is having what amounts to a bad dream, and he doesn't know what to make of it. He calls his advisors, the chief priests and the scribes, and asks them if they know where the Messiah is to be born. They look it up: "In Bethlehem," they say. "The prophet says so, right here."

Nebuchadnezzar, at least, was direct in his demands: *Tell me my dream and interpret it, or I'll have you killed.* Herod is more stealthy, sly. He calls for the wise men secretly and tells them this lie: "Go and search diligently for the child; and when you have found him, bring me word so that I may also go and pay homage." But we know King Herod will not bow before the little King born in Bethlehem.

Notice that King Herod doesn't question the authenticity of the star. He doesn't question the authenticity of the Scripture. But he is so certain of his own importance that he won't even go with the magi to see the child for himself. He is so busy safeguarding his own power that he won't even go and see the one who may be the long-awaited Messiah. He would rather stay in Jerusalem, send others to do his bidding, turn his magi guests into servants—*go, do this and that, and then come back and tell me.* He prefers secondhand hearsay rather than risk losing his power, his place as the fixed point of his own universe around which everything else must turn. What impoverishment we see when we look at Herod. He isn't searching for the Messiah, and so would completely miss this wondrous event

A God We Can See, Hear, Taste, and Touch

if the magi hadn't come to him. Herod isn't seeking God's truth, and so he spends his time and energy scheming and deceiving.

How different is the way of the magi. They are willing to seek everywhere—for signs in the sky, the palace of the king in Jerusalem—to find the King they seek. Their way is marked by joy, not fear. They come and go as they need to, following the truth where it leads. When they find the true King, they worship. They kneel before the Christ child, their gesture a symbol of submission and surrender to the one they adore. They offer gifts that symbolize their faith in Jesus as King: gold, for his royalty; frankincense, for his divinity; myrrh, for the sacrifice he would make on behalf of all people.

Herod is stuck. Herod is frozen to a spot from which he dare not move, lest all he holds dear comes crumbling down around him. Fear and anxiety keep him immobilized. The magi are a picture of movement—seeking, following, going, asking, finding, rejoicing, kneeling, worshipping, opening, offering. Joy and the pursuit of divine truth keep them going. Not frantic movement, but guided, studied, thoughtful, informed advancement, and a willingness to stop when they have found Jesus.

When these wise men use another of their magi abilities—the ability to interpret dreams—they heed the warning they received in a dream and go home by another way. A picture of spiritual peace, they give no assistance to Herod. They will not be caught up in his intrigues. They are free to seek, accept guidance, worship, and then free to go.

Which way do we choose: King Herod's or the way of the magi?

Let's be honest. None of us would cast ourselves in the role of Herod. But, really, have we ever felt threatened by something new? Ever thought that your authority would be diminished if someone else had authority too? Ever used someone, or attempted to use someone? Ever told even a small fib to keep your own self-image or position or power intact? Ever chosen to stay put over taking a risk, a risk that might mean change or being changed?

And the way of the magi is not easy. They made a commitment to study, to seek, to discern, to accept guidance. These magi were rooted in an ancient tradition, and yet were open to encountering the God of Israel, the God of the Hebrew Scriptures, the Most High "who has sovereignty over the kingdoms of mortals." They were willing to set out on a long journey and pay attention as they traveled.

The magi were rewarded with finding what they were searching for, submission to the only one worth that honor and pure, overwhelming joy.

First Sunday after the Epiphany: Baptism of Our Lord, Year A—Isaiah 42:1–9

> Here is my servant, whom I uphold,
> my chosen, in whom my soul delights;
> I have put my spirit upon him;
> he will bring forth justice to the nations.
> He will not cry or lift up his voice,
> or make it heard in the street;
> a bruised reed he will not break,
> and a dimly burning wick he will not quench;
> he will faithfully bring forth justice.
> He will not grow faint or be crushed
> until he has established justice in the earth;
> and the coastlands wait for his teaching.
> Thus says God, the Lord,
> who created the heavens and stretched them out,
> who spread out the earth and what comes from it,
> who gives breath to the people upon it
> and spirit to those who walk in it:
> I am the Lord, I have called you in righteousness,
> I have taken you by the hand and kept you;
> I have given you as a covenant to the people,
> a light to the nations,
> to open the eyes that are blind,
> to bring out the prisoners from the dungeon,
> from the prison those who sit in darkness.
> I am the Lord, that is my name;

my glory I give to no other,
nor my praise to idols.
See, the former things have come to pass,
and new things I now declare;
before they spring forth,
I tell you of them. (NRSV)

Acts 10:34–43

Then Peter began to speak to them: "I truly understand that God shows no partiality, but in every nation anyone who fears him and does what is right is acceptable to him. You know the message he sent to the people of Israel, preaching peace by Jesus Christ—he is Lord of all. That message spread throughout Judea, beginning in Galilee after the baptism that John announced: how God anointed Jesus of Nazareth with the Holy Spirit and with power; how he went about doing good and healing all who were oppressed by the devil, for God was with him. We are witnesses to all that he did both in Judea and in Jerusalem. They put him to death by hanging him on a tree; but God raised him on the third day and allowed him to appear, not to all the people but to us who were chosen by God as witnesses, and who ate and drank with him after he rose from the dead. He commanded us to preach to the people and to testify that he is the one ordained by God as judge of the living and the dead. All the prophets testify about him that everyone who believes in him receives forgiveness of sins through his name." (NRSV)

Matthew 3:13–17

Jesus came from Galilee to John at the Jordan, to be baptized by him. John would have prevented him, saying, "I need to be baptized by you, and do you come to me?" But Jesus answered him, "Let it be so now; for it is proper for us in this way to fulfill all righteousness." Then he consented. And when Jesus had been baptized, just as he came up from the water, suddenly the heavens were opened to him and he saw the Spirit of God descending like a dove and alighting on him. And a voice from heaven said, "This is my Son, the Beloved, with whom I am well pleased." (NRSV)

Love in Flesh and Bone

Red Rover, Red Rover, We Call . . .

  Amy E. Richter

I'm guessing that if you were good at sports as a child, you remember without angst a particular ritual from your grade school years. If, like me, you weren't necessarily an asset to a team's chances at victory, you might remember this tradition instead with a flutter in your stomach, a heightening of your heartbeat, or the desire to see a crevice open up at your feet wide enough so you could jump in and disappear. Whether first or last chosen, you know the tradition I mean: the captains of each team look over the crowd of children and one by one choose the kids they want. The big kids get chosen first, the ones we all know are great at the game. Then the average kids, or the ones that don't look like they'll be too much of a liability. Eventually, it's the weak, the small, the slow, the uncoordinated who are left standing there, hoping to be chosen, hoping not to be the last one left, the one who will make the team only because the gym teacher said that everyone has to end up on a side. Perhaps you know the anxiety that comes from wondering when your name will be called, whether you'll be the last one standing there unwanted.

I remember that in Vacation Bible School, during game time, one of the games we played was Red Rover. Do you know it? One team forms a human chain by linking hands and then stands across the field from another team that is formed into a human chain. The first team calls, "Red Rover, Red Rover, we call *Sandra* over." And the person called from the other team lets go from her human chain, runs across the field, and tries to run through one of the links in the other team's chain. If she can run through the link, she gets to take one of the people whose hands she's run through back with her to her team. If she gets stopped, she joins the opponent's team. Then it's the other team's turn to try to build their team by choosing and calling someone by name, and trying to hold on tight enough to gain another person for their side.

A God We Can See, Hear, Taste, and Touch

I remember that one of the older children at church, a teenager whose name was Rob, was one of the team captains. When picking his team, though, Rob did an unexpected thing. Rob kept picking the little kids, the weakest kids, the kids everyone knew were usually the last ones without a team to belong to. I remember the surprise: "You mean *me*? You want *me*?" "Yes, c'mon. I choose you. Get over here."

Now, would this team of the small and the weak strike fear into the hearts of the other team? Would this team ever go on to win the Super Bowl of Red Rover? Not a chance. But that wasn't the point. The point was to have fun and run around, to hear people call you by name, and then run as fast as you could toward people waiting for you on the other side of the field. In fact, the game was won when eventually everyone formed one big team, one long line where everyone was included, caught by people whose hands, when held together, could hold you too. That was the point, and Rob's choosing worked.

I have no idea where Rob is now. But I hope he's still doing something to choose the weak and the small, and to make them feel wanted.

Today we hear the story of Jesus' baptism. When Jesus first comes to John to be baptized, John the Baptist responds like one of Rob's unlikely Red Rover picks: "You mean *me*? Me, baptize *you*? It should be the other way around!" "Trust me," says Jesus. "This is right. In fact, it's not just right—it's righteousness." God is doing amazing things, reconciling all the world to God and one another through Jesus, and through the unlikely choices Jesus makes. "Who me?" asks John. "Yes, you," says Jesus. John would be the first of many unlikely people Jesus would choose to help him bring God's promises to fruition. "I want you—yes, *you*—to do this for me." *C'mon, get over to my team.*

Jesus knew about being chosen and choosing others. Jesus was baptized, and when he comes up out of the water, the Spirit of God descends on him like a dove. And a voice from heaven says, "This is my Son, the Beloved, with whom I am well pleased."

These words are meant to help us remember the message from Isaiah: "Here is my servant, my chosen, in whom my soul delights."

Jesus is the one whom Isaiah describes, the one who comes to establish justice on the earth, who will be a light to the nations, who will open the eyes that are blind, bring out the prisoners from the dungeon.

But, surprise! This servant of God will not use force to do these things. "He will not cry or lift up his voice. He will not break a bruised reed. He will not quench a dimly burning wick" (Isa 42:1–3). No, this one who comes to liberate us from all captivity of body, mind, and spirit will exercise a completely different style of power. He will establish justice, not by violence or coercion, not by the power that snaps off tender twigs or snuffs out small flames, but by persistent strength through suffering: "He will not grow faint or be crushed until he has established justice in the earth" (42:4). This is Jesus, God's beloved Son, God's chosen servant, chosen to do God's will of bringing freedom and justice for all people.

After Jesus is baptized, he goes out into the desert. He confronts and overcomes Satan, and then is ready to get to work. He starts by choosing his team. The gospel shows us the beginnings of his team-building. Jesus chooses fishermen, tax collectors, mothers and mothers-in-law, children, prostitutes, zealots, people he healed, one man who would betray Jesus to his enemies, one who will deny he even knew Jesus in his hour of deepest need, people who didn't really get what he was talking about, or didn't try to follow his teachings until after he was raised from the dead, and some who still doubted even then. Apparently Jesus chose people to follow him, not for their brains or brawn or courage, but because Jesus loved them. He loved them, and he wanted them to be on his team. *Who me?* Yes, you.

So, can just anybody be on Jesus' team? Would Jesus choose just anyone? The fact that Jesus may include me if I don't have to be perfect is comforting. But when we consider who else we may find ourselves holding hands with, it can get a little uncomfortable.

Peter found this out, as we discovered today in our reading from Acts. In the story that comes before today's reading, Peter is told by a messenger of God to go visit a man named Cornelius, a man Peter has never met, a man who loves God, gives alms generously, prays regularly, but needs more information about God. A

A God We Can See, Hear, Taste, and Touch

man who from the sounds of it would be just Peter's type of guy, Peter's next best friend, a natural kind of person for Peter to associate with. Except for one thing: Peter is a Jew; Cornelius is a Gentile. And not just any Gentile. A Roman, and a military officer, one of those stationed in the area to keep the Jews under control. There they are: Jew and Gentile; subject and enforcer; and yet two people who love God, two people to whom God has reached out, two people who would both be changed because God has brought them together. God opens Peter's heart. And so Peter hears that he should share the good news of Jesus with Cornelius, should baptize him, should accept Cornelius and his entire household as God's beloved children, and should welcome them as his own brothers and sisters in Christ. God opens Cornelius's heart. And so Cornelius listens to Peter and hears the good news of Jesus.

What is revealed to Peter through this event is described in today's reading. Peter says, "I truly understand that God shows no partiality, but in every nation anyone who fears him and does what is right is acceptable to him. You know the message he sent to the people of Israel, preaching peace by Jesus Christ—he is Lord of all" (Acts 10:34-36). God shows no partiality. God draws close to all, loves all, treasures all, wants all, pursues all.

The climax of the story is that Cornelius is baptized after he has heard Peter's testimony about Jesus. Please note, Peter proclaims that he understands that God shows no partiality before Cornelius is baptized, not after. God's love for all is proclaimed quite apart from baptism. Baptism is the sign and seal that we accept the love of God, the kind of love that breaks down the barriers we would set between us. As Paul wrote to the Galatians, "As many of you as were baptized into Christ have clothed yourselves with Christ. There is no longer Jew or Greek, slave or free, there is no longer male and female; for you are all one in Christ Jesus" (Gal 3:27-28). The baptized are people who try to live their lives in the knowledge that God, who shows no partiality, invites everyone to be on the team, and, eventually, through the grace, mercy, forgiveness, and love of God in Jesus Christ, all may be one. God loves our particularities, loves the diversity of humanity and all creation, celebrates our uniqueness, but God refuses to use those distinctions as reasons not to choose us and everyone else.

If God in Jesus wants all, chooses all, draws close to all, then how we treat one another must be affected. As Episcopal bishop and theologian Tom Breidenthal writes, "The purpose of the Incarnation was not to rescue us from nearness . . . but to set our nearness right. Through the Incarnation the Word of God has become our neighbor. As our neighbor, Jesus reveals to us what nearness looks like when it is not corrupted by sin, and bestows on everyone who receives him the experience of a redeemed and justified nearness. We are encouraged by this experience to begin . . . to embrace our nearness with one another."[9] God shows no partiality: God draws near to all and, in Jesus, as flesh and blood, is radically near to all—and wants us to be near to one another too.

God, in Jesus Christ, has already called you by name. If you have been baptized, then you have already said yes to God's all-encompassing love and to being part of God's gathering of us all.

Second Sunday after the Epiphany, Year C—
Isaiah 62:1–5

> For Zion's sake I will not keep silent, and for Jerusalem's sake I will not rest until her vindication shines out like the dawn, and her salvation like a burning torch. The nations shall see your vindication, and all the kings your glory; and you shall be called by a new name that the mouth of the LORD will give. You shall be a crown of beauty in the hand of the LORD, and a royal diadem in the hand of your God. You shall no more be termed Forsaken, and your land shall no more be termed Desolate; but you shall be called My Delight Is in Her, and your land Married; for the LORD delights in you, and your land shall be married. For as a young man marries a young woman, so shall your builder marry you, and as the bridegroom rejoices over the bride, so shall your God rejoice over you. (NRSV)

---

9. Breidenthal, *Christian Households*, 31.

A God We Can See, Hear, Taste, and Touch

JOHN 2:1–11

> On the third day there was a wedding in Cana of Galilee, and the mother of Jesus was there. Jesus and his disciples had also been invited to the wedding. When the wine gave out, the mother of Jesus said to him, "They have no wine." And Jesus said to her, "Woman, what concern is that to you and to me? My hour has not yet come." His mother said to the servants, "Do whatever he tells you." Now standing there were six stone water jars for the Jewish rites of purification, each holding twenty or thirty gallons. Jesus said to them, "Fill the jars with water." And they filled them up to the brim. He said to them, "Now draw some out, and take it to the chief steward." So they took it. When the steward tasted the water that had become wine, and did not know where it came from (though the servants who had drawn the water knew), the steward called the bridegroom and said to him, "Everyone serves the good wine first, and then the inferior wine after the guests have become drunk. But you have kept the good wine until now." Jesus did this, the first of his signs, in Cana of Galilee, and revealed his glory; and his disciples believed in him. (NRSV)

A Sign from God

 Amy E. Richter

Wow! The first of Jesus' signs—what the other Gospels call "miracles"—was turning water into wine. His first sign that indicated his identity and inspired faith was not healing a sick person, bringing someone back from the dead, forgiving sins, or exorcising a demon. It was making gallons and gallons of wine, about one hundred and fifty, and making a party last longer. Is Jesus just one cool savior, or is his first miracle a little trivial?

Maybe this sign is not about Jesus loving a good party, although by all accounts he did. His opponents called him a glutton and a drunkard, and he often got in trouble for sharing table fellowship with the wrong kind of people. And maybe this sign is not just trivial, or the person who wrote the Gospel of John wouldn't have used one of his big words, "sign," for it. The other things John calls "signs" include healing the sick, raising people from the dead, feeding a multitude on five loaves and two fish, and Jesus' appearing resurrected from the dead among his amazed disciples. So "signs" are big, important, meaningful, reality-shifting events.

How is making a ridiculous amount of wine at a small-town wedding reception on par with raising the dead, feeding the hungry, walking through locked doors to show the scars on his hands and feet and side and proclaim that death has been defeated? As a "sign," what does it point to? What makes this wine so important?

Wine did not flow freely for most of the people who lived in Jesus' time. Many peasants were involved in its production, but few people drank it on a regular basis. Cheese and bread and olive oil were the daily fare of most people. Most people drank water, not wine, when they were thirsty. At a wedding or another big family celebration, it was different. This was a time for wine, a time to spend scarce money on the rarer things of life. A time to share food and drink that was special. And because wine was not something everyone had a glass of with their dinner, because it was something connected with special times and celebrations, it was a great sign in the Bible of the heavenly banquet, the eschatological—or last times—feast at the end of time as we know it.

For example, listen to the prophet Isaiah's description of the age to come, the promised fulfillment of God's plans and dreams for the end of time:

"On this mountain the LORD of hosts will make for all peoples a feast of rich food, a feast of well-matured wines, of rich food filled with marrow, of well-matured wines strained clear. And he will destroy on this mountain the shroud that is cast over all peoples, the sheet that is spread over all nations; he will swallow up death for ever. Then the LORD GOD will wipe away the tears from all faces, and the disgrace of his people he will take away from all the earth, for the LORD has spoken" (Isa 25:6–8).

This is Isaiah's image for the end of time, when all is brought to its fulfillment: an end to tears, a clear manifestation of God, and a great feast for all peoples, a feast of really good meat, rich, fatty food, and wine better than the best you've ever tasted. Furthermore,

A God We Can See, Hear, Taste, and Touch

as we heard in our first lesson, also from Isaiah, a bride and a bridegroom and the delight and rejoicing they share are symbols of God's joy over God's people.

So when Jesus makes gallons and gallons of wine at a wedding reception, it's a sign—it's pointing to the scriptural promises that God will bring all people to God's own self, that God will pour down God's love and the abundance of God's joy on all people, that the perfection that lies in God's great future is real. But more—that the future abundance and grace and joy has begun in Jesus Christ. The future is now, the glory and grace and love of God are available now.

That's why turning water into wine is the first of the signs Jesus did. This is why the rest of the signs follow. This first sign is saying, "Look! God's future is breaking in now, has begun now in Jesus." What else does God's future look like? It looks like hungry people being fed, sick people being healed, dead people being raised from death, death itself being defeated.

God's future is available now. In the present. In this life. And we can trust that God will keep God's promises for the end of time, because Jesus already brought in the possibility of joy and hope and new life now, even in this world, where perfection is not yet complete, where perfect wholeness still lies ahead. But trust Jesus—it is real. God will keep God's promises.

So, how do we participate in this new life, God's perfect, joy-filled future that is available now?

Mary gives the answer: "Do whatever he tells you." Seek life at its source. Seek joy at its source. Seek to know what Jesus Christ asks of you. This is the essence of discipleship. This is the key for joining Jesus in his new way of being in the world. This is the key: do whatever he tells you.

Perhaps it is significant to know who the people were who knew how the water had turned into wine. The people who recognized, up close, with their own eyes, the amazing thing happening in front of them, were the servants. The ones who did what Jesus told them to do. While everyone else around them was caught up in whatever was going on at the party, the servants got to witness a miracle.

They even got to help make it happen. They got to have a hand in Jesus' first sign. They were there, doing the mundane task of filling water jugs with water. They were just doing what Jesus told them to do: "Now draw some out and take it . . . So they took it." They just did the simple, straightforward things Jesus told them to do, and they got to participate in a miracle.

Do whatever Jesus tells you. Water becomes the finest wine. The mundane becomes miraculous.

Jesus tells us all some very simple, straightforward things to do. There are lots of verbs in the Gospels, commands, instructions that really aren't even that hard to understand when it comes right down to it, that are about simple obedience. Jesus tells us to do things: love, share, give, serve, listen, learn, worship, pray.

God even gives us particulars, contexts and jobs and families, a community, and a church family in which to be obedient. Love *him*. Love *her*. Love *them*. Share your money, your time, your particular gift, your ability with *that child*, with *that elder*, with *that family*. Worship with this parish family. Pray at your desk, at your bedside, with your teenager, for your spouse, your partner, your parent. Listen for what Jesus tells you to do. Do it. You may participate in a miracle, you may get a glimpse, a sign of God's perfect future, a sign of God's heavenly feast, even right here, right now.

THIRD SUNDAY AFTER THE EPIPHANY, YEAR C—
LUKE 4:14–21

> Jesus, filled with the power of the Spirit, returned to Galilee, and a report about him spread through all the surrounding country. He began to teach in their synagogues and was praised by everyone. When he came to Nazareth, where he had been brought up, he went to the synagogue on the sabbath day, as was his custom. He stood up to read, and the scroll of the prophet Isaiah was given to him. He unrolled the scroll and found the place where it was written:
>
> > "The Spirit of the Lord is upon me,
> > because he has anointed me
> > to bring good news to the poor.

A God We Can See, Hear, Taste, and Touch

> He has sent me to proclaim release to the captives
> and recovery of sight to the blind,
> to let the oppressed go free,
> to proclaim the year of the Lord's favor."
>
> And he rolled up the scroll, gave it back to the attendant, and sat down. The eyes of all in the synagogue were fixed on him. Then he began to say to them, "Today this scripture has been fulfilled in your hearing." (NRSV)

Exile and Return

 Joseph S. Pagano

One of the central ways people have described the human condition is in terms of exile and return, captivity and release. And these images do seem to characterize well our human experiences of longing for something more, and for release from our present circumstances. We may long for something in the past, a memory of past life or past love, or we may long for something in the future, a hope for a new life or a new love. We are always hoping, always yearning, always longing for something that seems to lie just beyond our grasp. Exile is a good metaphor for this: separated from that to which we belong, that which we hold dear, that which we remember, that which we yearn for. And what keeps us separated is often experienced as a captivity or bondage. The captivity of grinding poverty and social circumstances that diminish so many lives. The captivity of illness and disease that cause us to feel betrayed by our own bodies. The captivity of anger and grudges and the inability to forgive that cause our souls to shrivel and turns us sour and cold. The captivity of fear that co-opts us into building our own walls of imprisonment, both physical and emotional. To be human is in so many ways to be an exile, a captive, and to long for release and return.

The themes of exile and return, captivity and release, are found throughout Western literature. Homer's *Odyssey* tells the story of Odysseus's return home to his beloved Penelope after spending ten years fighting the Trojan War. It takes Odysseus years to make it home, and his journey is not an easy one. Along the way there are trials and temptations, shipwrecks and monsters. But he finally makes it home, discloses his identity in the contest with his bow, and is restored to his wife, Penelope. Dante's *Divine Comedy* is the story of the Pilgrim's journey through the Inferno, the Purgatorio, and finally through Paradise. What begins with the Pilgrim lost in a dark forest ends in the realm of light, in the vision of God. And in that modern day classic *The Wizard of Oz*, we have the story of Dorothy's journey from Kansas, to the Land of Oz, and then back again. Along the way there are the Munchkins, friends like the Scarecrow and the Tin Man, and the yellow brick road. This story contains one of the most enduring images of the human condition that I know: the Cowardly Lion, his feet bound with rope and his face streaming with tears, trembles in fear while the flying monkeys who have bound him hover in the background.

In all these stories, human life is seen as a journey. To be human is to find yourself somewhere along the way: somewhere at sea with Odysseus, somewhere between a dark wood and paradise with Dante, or somewhere along the Yellow Brick Road with Dorothy. We are all traveling somewhere. We all live somewhere between exile and return, captivity and release.

In our gospel lesson for today, Jesus is in the synagogue of his home town. He stands up, is given the scroll of the prophet Isaiah, finds this passage, and reads: "The Spirit of the Lord is upon me, because he has anointed me to bring good news to the poor. He has sent me to proclaim release to the captives and recovery of sight to the blind, to let the oppressed go free, to proclaim the year of the Lord's favor" (Isa 61:1-2). Then he sits back down and says, "Today this scripture has been fulfilled in your hearing" (Luke 4:21).

The passages from Isaiah that Jesus read were written just after the Babylonian exile came to an end. The Babylonian exile was one of the most devastating experiences in the history of Israel. In 587 BCE, the Babylonians moved south into Judea and crushed the Jewish people, destroyed the temple, and carried many of them back to Babylon. It would be hard to overestimate how devastating this was for the Jews. Their sense of identity as a people was tied to

A God We Can See, Hear, Taste, and Touch

the promised land, the land that God had given them. Their temple was the sign and site of God's presence with his people. Now these things were gone. Their homeland was razed, their temple was destroyed and they were carried off to a foreign land. How would they understand themselves as the people of God? The words of Psalm 137 capture this sense of exile with great poignancy: "By the waters of Babylon we sat down and wept, when we remembered you, O Zion. As for our harps, we hung them up on the trees in the midst of that land. For those who led us away captive asked us for a song, and our oppressors called for mirth: 'Sing us one of the songs of Zion.' How shall we sing the LORD's song upon an alien soil?" (Ps 137:1–4).

We feel the sense of yearning and longing in this psalm. Living in exile, by the waters of Babylon, the Jews sat down and wept when they remembered their home. Their captors said, *sing us one of your native songs*. But how could they sing the Lord's song in a foreign land? In the midst of exile, they remember Jerusalem, they remember their homeland, remember that they belong in a different place, remember that they belong to God. By the waters of Babylon, the people sat down and wept when they remembered their home.

To this captive people, to this people returning from exile, the prophet Isaiah spoke comforting words, words of hope, words of deliverance: "The Spirit of the Lord is upon me, because he has anointed me to bring good news to the poor. He has sent me to proclaim release to the captives and recovery of sight to the blind, to let the oppressed go free, to proclaim the year of the Lord's favor." In the midst of exile, in the midst of captivity, in the midst of tears, God speaks words of comfort and hope. The time of exile is coming to an end, and the Jews will be able to go home.

What does it feel like to be released from captivity, to return from exile? It feels like good news to the poor. Like the blind recovering their sight. Like the oppressed being set free. It feels like hope in the midst of our longing. It feels like God making a way out of no way. It feels like going home.

In our gospel lesson Jesus reads these words from Isaiah and says, "Today this Scripture has been fulfilled" (Luke 4:21). It's an amazing claim. Today, in your midst, in your hearing, these promises are being fulfilled. Jesus takes the words about the return from exile from the prophet Isaiah and says that God's rescue of God's people is happening in Jesus' life and ministry. It is the good news that so many people in Jesus' day were longing for. And yet, and as is so often the case, Jesus fulfills these promises in shocking and surprising ways. The poor and the dispossessed, the blind and the captive will include Gentiles as well as Jews, will include all those who are impoverished, will include all those who are marginalized from fellowship with God and neighbor, all those who are outcasts. It is a claim that will shock the sensibilities of many of Jesus' contemporaries. But it is also the essence of the gospel, the good news of God for all people, that will be carried out in Jesus' life and ministry: his healing of the blind, his feeding of the hungry, his welcoming of the stranger, his freeing of those who are in captivity, his teaching of forgiveness, and his stretching out of his arms of love on the hard wood of the cross so that all may come within his saving embrace. Freedom. Release. Recovery. Good news for the whole world!

We all live in some sort of exile. We all live in some type of captivity. Captive to the pain of physical illness. Captive to financial burdens. Captive to dead-end jobs. Captive to broken relationships. Captive to drugs and alcohol. Captive to grief over the loss of a loved one. Captive to fear and loneliness. Captive to what other people think of us. Captive to anger. Captive to the inability to forgive. We are all held captive by something, and we all long for release from our bondage. We all long for an end of our exile.

The good news is that God offers us release from our captivity in the life, death, and resurrection of Jesus Christ. Now how does this happen? Quite frankly, I don't know if I can say much more than by the grace and mercy of God. And again, to be honest, I can't say that it always happens, at least in ways that are perceivable by these all-too-human eyes. And yet, and yet, I have seen the Lord deliver people from what was holding them captive enough times to know that it can happen. I have seen people delivered from their addiction to drugs and alcohol who have gone on to lead beautiful lives. I have seen people delivered from the grip of terrible depression who have found real joy and real peace. I have seen people who

A God We Can See, Hear, Taste, and Touch

lost a beloved spouse find new life and new love. I have seen people let go of their anger and their hurt and forgive. I have seen enemies become friends. I have seen people who came from impoverished circumstances learn and succeed and give back to their communities. I have seen people in prison let go of death-dealing patterns of behavior and learn new ways and embrace life. I have seen people healed and forgiven by the power of the cross. I have seen all these things, which is to say, I have seen gospel, the good news of God's love for all people in Jesus Christ.

For us and for our salvation. To free us from any captivity. To help us navigate the tricky waters of our earthly journey. To heal us from our sickness unto death. To bring us from the darkness of the woods into the brightness of God's eternal light. To protect us from flying monkeys. To offer to all people deliverance from exile and the promise of a heavenly home.

The Spirit of the Lord anointed Jesus to bring the good news to the poor, to the blind, to the captive, to the oppressed, to us, in our hearing, in our lives, on this day!

FOURTH SUNDAY AFTER THE EPIPHANY, YEAR C—
1 CORINTHIANS 13:1–13

> If I speak in the tongues of mortals and of angels, but do not have love, I am a noisy gong or a clanging cymbal. And if I have prophetic powers, and understand all mysteries and all knowledge, and if I have all faith, so as to remove mountains, but do not have love, I am nothing. If I give away all my possessions, and if I hand over my body so that I may boast, but do not have love, I gain nothing. Love is patient; love is kind; love is not envious or boastful or arrogant or rude. It does not insist on its own way; it is not irritable or resentful; it does not rejoice in wrongdoing, but rejoices in the truth. It bears all things, believes all things, hopes all things, endures all things. Love never ends. But as for prophecies, they will come to an end; as for tongues, they will cease; as for knowledge, it will come to an end. For we know only in part, and we prophesy only in part; but when the complete comes, the partial will come to an end. When I was a child, I spoke like a child, I thought like a child, I reasoned like a child; when I became an adult, I put an end to childish ways. For now we see in a mirror,

dimly, but then we will see face to face. Now I know only in part; then I will know fully, even as I have been fully known. And now faith, hope, and love abide, these three; and the greatest of these is love. (NRSV)

What Love Does and Doesn't

 Amy E. Richter

Few passages are so beloved and frequently heard at weddings as our reading today from 1 Corinthians. Love is patient; love is kind. Love is not envious or boastful or rude.

I once heard this passage read at a wedding as if it were a personal address from the older sister who was reading it to her younger brother. She clearly thought her kid brother, who was about to become a husband, needed some special guidance that she was not sure he was capable of receiving: "Love is patient, *Larry*. Love is kind, *Larry*. It's not envious, or boastful, or rude, *Larry*." *Larry. Got that?*

The reader was right about one thing—this passage is personal. These are words meant to be taken to heart. But they are not just for grooms, not just for brides. In fact, the original context was not marriage at all, but Christian community as a whole. St. Paul was addressing a church when he wrote these words, the church in the city of Corinth. It was a church that had its difficulties.

Corinth was a prosperous city, a seaport, a center for shipping, commerce, industry, and government. It was a city of self-made people, people who thrived in business, trade, law, and all the professions that go with being part of a successful community. Along with economic success came opportunities for squandering money, for pleasure-seeking in immoral ways. Corinth also had its poor and its working class, all of the people whose labor is necessary to make things go: the servants, staff, day laborers, and wage earners.

The Corinthians brought their differences with them to church as well, and not in a good, "let's celebrate diversity" kind of way. Paul had to tell them that the church should be different from the city

A God We Can See, Hear, Taste, and Touch

outside. Outside, people think boasting, taking advantage of others, and treating people differently based on their social class is fine. Outside, people think it's okay that some people have more than enough to eat while others go hungry. Outside, people don't bat an eye over drunkenness and adultery. Outside, being self-centered is part of the game; climbing the ladder and using people on the way up is just par for the course.

Church, says Paul, is different. Church is the body of Christ. We are all a part of it, all connected one to another, whether we acknowledge our interdependence or not. There is no unimportant part of the body. There is no place for boasting, or treating one part of the body well and another part poorly. There is no place for misusing the body. And you can't divide up the body, cut parts off, and expect the body to thrive, or even survive.

Paul had to remind this church, with all its little factions, on the brink of divide, living in ways that no one would ever guess its members were followers of Jesus Christ, of the basics: It's about love. It's all about love. Love is not just for those inside the church—love is for those outside the church too. But how are they going to know about love outside the church if we don't even know about love inside the church? If we, inside the church, can experience love and be loving toward one another, then we might just be able to transform the world outside too. If we will allow God to transform us through love, maybe God will use us to help God in the work of transforming the whole world.

The basics, the foundation: What is love?

Love is patient, kind. Love is not envious or boastful or arrogant or rude. Love does not insist on its own way. It is not irritable or resentful. Love does not rejoice in wrongdoing. It rejoices in the truth. Love bears all things, believes all things, hopes all things, endures all things. Love never ends.

That's how a community is when it's based on love. Whether it's a small community of a bride and a groom, whose falling in love gives them a sense of awe and wonder, a sense that somehow they are participating in something much larger than themselves, that somehow through being true to each other they are participating in something of cosmic significance; or whether it's a large church community, a church large enough that if all the people actually gathered for worship all at the same time on the same day they couldn't fit in one place, and yet as a church, connected to one another, as a body made up of many members—whether two or three or a hundred or a thousand gathered in the name of Jesus—the description of love is the same: patient, kind, not arrogant, not envious or boastful or rude, not irritable or resentful.

Paul wrote in Greek, and his description of love is all in terms of verbs. We have to use some adjectives in English. This is what love does and does not do. Love is grand, majestic, powerful, the most important thing. But it is not beyond us. We are swept into its powerful and potent grasp, or not. Love is what we do, or don't do. Love is shown in the choices we make about how we behave toward one another. Love comes with a whole bunch of ways to reflect on what we do and say: Am I being boastful? Was I being rude? What would be the kind thing to do? What if I respond with patience? How can we rejoice in the truth? What would it mean to be a community that loves through hope and endurance?

We are a church community, St. Anne's Parish, with the same holy mission of the church through the ages: proclaim the good news of God's love for all in Jesus Christ. We are the Church in the Circle in Annapolis, Maryland. Our geographic location reminds us that we are encircled by the love of God. Our mission is to trust, proclaim, teach, and celebrate that God surrounds us, enfolds us, and the whole world with divine love. We gather as a church community, we come into Church Circle to be transformed, forgiven, reminded of love, nurtured by love, and to practice love in how we treat one another so that we can go out from Church Circle to show God's love to others too. So others may see our church family, us, gathered as the brothers and sisters of Jesus Christ, the sons and daughters of God, and say, *see how they love one another.*

Here's how another translation of 1 Corinthians 13 puts what others could see in us: "Love is never selfish, never quick to take offense. Love keeps no score of wrongs, takes no pleasure in the sins of others, but delights in the truth. There is nothing love cannot face; there is no limit to its faith, its hope, its endurance" (Revised English Bible, 13:4–8).

A God We Can See, Hear, Taste, and Touch

God is love, we are told in the Bible (1 John 4:8). So our loving is not just a matter of applying ourselves, trying hard, hoping it goes well. When we love, we participate in the divine life. We love because God first loved us. Allowing God's love to take root in us, shape us, show in us, flow through us, means that we have a never-failing source of love from which to draw. Love never ends.

So take this beautiful lesson from 1 Corinthians personally. God does not pronounce these words to you as an older sibling at a wedding, unsure of whether you are up to the task or capable of grasping the concept. Take these words as a description of God's love for you, God's intention toward you: God is patient. God is kind. God is not selfish, not quick to take offense. God keeps no score of wrongs, takes no pleasure in sin but delights in the truth. There is nothing God cannot face; there is no limit to God's faith, God's hope, God's endurance.

Now faith and hope and love abide. And the greatest of these is love.

FIFTH SUNDAY AFTER THE EPIPHANY, YEAR C—ISAIAH 6:1–8

> In the year that King Uzziah died, I saw the Lord sitting on a throne, high and lofty; and the hem of his robe filled the temple. Seraphs were in attendance above him; each had six wings: with two they covered their faces, and with two they covered their feet, and with two they flew. And one called to another and said:
>
> "Holy, holy, holy is the LORD of hosts;
> the whole earth is full of his glory."
>
> The pivots on the thresholds shook at the voices of those who called, and the house filled with smoke. And I said: "Woe is me! I am lost, for I am a man of unclean lips, and I live among a people of unclean lips; yet my eyes have seen the King, the LORD of hosts!"
>
> Then one of the seraphs flew to me, holding a live coal that had been taken from the altar with a pair of tongs. The seraph touched my mouth with it and said: "Now that this has touched your lips, your guilt has departed and your sin is blotted out." Then I heard the voice of the Lord saying, "Whom shall I send, and who will go for us?" And I said, "Here am I; send me!" (NRSV)

Love in Flesh and Bone

LUKE 5:1–11

> Once while Jesus was standing beside the lake of Gennesaret, and the crowd was pressing in on him to hear the word of God, he saw two boats there at the shore of the lake; the fishermen had gone out of them and were washing their nets. He got into one of the boats, the one belonging to Simon, and asked him to put out a little way from the shore. Then he sat down and taught the crowds from the boat. When he had finished speaking, he said to Simon, "Put out into the deep water and let down your nets for a catch." Simon answered, "Master, we have worked all night long but have caught nothing. Yet if you say so, I will let down the nets." When they had done this, they caught so many fish that their nets were beginning to break. So they signaled their partners in the other boat to come and help them. And they came and filled both boats, so that they began to sink. But when Simon Peter saw it, he fell down at Jesus' knees, saying, "Go away from me, Lord, for I am a sinful man!" For he and all who were with him were amazed at the catch of fish that they had taken; and so also were James and John, sons of Zebedee, who were partners with Simon. Then Jesus said to Simon, "Do not be afraid; from now on you will be catching people." When they had brought their boats to shore, they left everything and followed him. (NRSV)

The Holy

 Joseph S. Pagano

Have you ever experienced some place or some thing that was holy? Have you ever felt yourself in the presence of something so stupendous that it is impossible to put into words? Maybe you ventured out late in the night to watch a meteor shower. On a clear night, lying on a blanket in a field or on the hood of your car, away from the ambient light of city or town, you gazed into the night sky looking for shooting stars. Then something happens as you turn your attention to the night sky for a prolonged period of time. Somehow the light from stars seems to draw near, almost pinning you to our

A God We Can See, Hear, Taste, and Touch

planet. You feel vast and tiny at the same time, your mind fills with awe at the immensity of space and your heart thrills with the sensation of being spun on the earth, circling the sun, floating in the Milky Way, expanding with the universe.

Have you ever walked into a Gothic cathedral and felt yourself hushed by the soaring space of the church? Did you feel like you should pause and walk reverently and speak softly, and, at the same time, did you feel drawn by the lines of the church to move more deeply into its mystery and presence?

Have you ever been in nature, perhaps hiking in the mountains, and come upon a sharp precipice with an amazing view of an adjacent mountain range and found yourself stopped dead in your tracks? Did you feel awed and silenced by the rugged beauty, and, at the same time, did you want to get as close to the edge of the cliff as you could so that you could move closer to the majesty of it all?

Have you ever been transformed by a great drama? Has a great work of art ever inspired in you the emotion of pity, and, at the same time, the emotion of terror?

If you've had experiences like these, then you may have had an experience of the holy. At least, that's what Rudolf Otto, the great scholar of religious experience, thought. Somehow, according to Otto, in the presence of the holy we are filled with great awe and reverence, and, at the same time, mysteriously fascinated and attracted by it. Otto described the experience of the holy with the Latin phrase *mysterium tremendum et fascinans*. Somehow, things always sound so much more important in Latin! The rough translation is that Otto sees the experience of the holy as the experience of a mystery that is both tremendous and fascinating. The *mystery* part is that to experience the holy is to experience something that lies beyond our human capacities to fully grasp or to comprehend it. It's not like a really hard math problem that someday, with lots of tutoring and hard work, you could solve. The holy, according to Otto, can never be grasped or solved. Rather, the holy is a mystery we can experience, a mystery we can encounter, a mystery that can transform us, but it is a mystery that always remains beyond our comprehension. In a certain sense we may be able to point to our experiences of holy, but we can never really grasp them. In the presence of holy mystery, we may find ourselves silent or speechless.

The *tremendous* part of the experience of the holy is that sense of dread and awe we feel in the presence of God. When the biblical writers talk about the "fear of the Lord," it is this experience they are talking about. They are not talking about fear in the way we are afraid of Jack the Ripper or frightened by a scene in a scary movie. The "fear of the Lord" is rather the sense of awe and reverence we feel in the presence of the divine. Otto says it is the feeling of "submergence into nothingness before an overpowering, absolute might."[10] The experience of the holy is so awesome, so majestic, so powerful, that in its presence we feel small, we feel submerged. We may feel like Job who, when he encounters God in the whirlwind, covers his mouth with his hands and is comforted that he is dust. In the presence of the divine, we may feel like bowing our heads and saying, "Holy, holy, holy Lord, God of power and might, heaven and earth are full of your glory, Hosanna in the highest."

But the experience of the holy is not only tremendous, it is also positively attractive. This is the *fascinating* part of the experience of the holy. Somehow, when we encounter the divine, we are enthralled or drawn to the mystery of God. The experience of the divine is not only awe inspiring but also positively attractive, even intoxicating. But it is more than the sense of warmth and comfort we get when our purring kitty crawls into our lap or when, on a cool evening, we crawl into our beds. That's the attraction of the warm and cuddly, not the holy that maintains a sense of awe and power, even as it draws us in. In the presence of the divine, we are transported into a heightened frame of consciousness and become filled with feelings of love, mercy, peace, and blessing. In the presence of the holy, we may feel like shouting, "Be joyful in the Lord, all you lands, serve the Lord with gladness, and come before his presence with a song."

Wordsworth once wrote: "I have felt / A presence that disturbs me with joy / Of elevated thoughts; a sense sublime / Of something far more deeply interfused, / Whose dwelling is the light of set-

---

10. Otto, *Idea of the Holy*, 10.

ting suns, / And the round ocean and the living air, / And the blue sky, and in the mind of man: / A motion and a spirit, that impels / All thinking things, all objects of all thought, And rolls through all things."[11] The experience of the holy. Mysterious. Tremendous. Fascinating. All at the same time. If you have felt a sense of a presence and a power that is beyond rational comprehension, which fills you with awe and reverence, and which also evokes fascination and irresistible desire, then you have had a sense of the holy.

I mention these experiences because in our Old Testament and gospel lessons for today, we have two classic texts on the holiness of God. Otto indeed describes the nature and dynamics of our encounter with the holy with great power and insight. But, as great as Otto's work is, it is not perfect. The problem, I think, comes partly from his method. To describe the idea of the holy, Otto looks to comparative religion and seeks the common essence in a variety of experiences, and in so doing strips away what is distinctive to each religious tradition. When it comes to the experiences of ancient Israel, however, this means relegating the moral dimension and the salvific purposes of God to a secondary level. This happens because Otto thinks that goodness and salvation are later additions to the idea of the holy. This just doesn't seem right. Moses' encounter with God in the burning bush seems as much about God's righteousness as it is about God's tremendousness and fascination. Moreover, God reveals himself to Moses for a reason: so that Moses can free God's people from bondage to the Egyptians. So yes, the God of Israel is mysterious, tremendous, and fascinating, but he also reveals himself as righteous and as savior. The holiness of the God of Israel is the holiness of the righteous savior.

In our Old Testament lesson, the prophet Isaiah has an awesome vision of the Lord. Isaiah is in the temple, taking part in the worship service. He looks from the sanctuary, which is filled with the smoke of incense and echoing with the sound of music, toward the innermost chamber of the Holy of Holies, when his vision of God occurs. He speaks of the experience of the tremendum of God, seated on a throne, high and lofty, with the hem of his robe filling

---

11. Wordsworth, "Lines Composed a Few Miles," 262.

the temple. It's an awe-inspiring experience of God, complete with angels who cry out, "Holy, holy, holy is the Lord of hosts; the whole earth is full of his glory." The building shakes as the voices fill the temple.

In the presence of the Lord, Isaiah is filled not only with a sense of smallness but also of his sinfulness. Yes, Isaiah is aware of his creaturely status before the Lord, but that doesn't fully account for what he says: "Woe is me! I am lost, for I am a man of unclean lips, and I live among a people of unclean lips; yet my eyes have seen the King, the Lord of hosts." The holiness of God is an ethical holiness. God is experienced as not only awesome and powerful, but also as righteous. In the presence of the holy God of Israel, Isaiah shakes with the awareness of being a creature—"I am a man"—and a sinner—"of unclean lips." He is literally overwhelmed by his encounter with the holy God.

But Isaiah's encounter with the Lord does not end here. The experience of the holy is not only tremendous but also fascinating. It doesn't just knock us over. It also lifts us up. As Isaiah explains, an angel comes to him and touches his lips with a live coal and tells him, "Now that this has touched your lips, your guilt has departed and your sin is blotted out." God's holiness is also shown in his gracious cleansing of Isaiah. God's holiness is experienced not only as a righteousness that reveals our sinfulness but also as a graciousness that blots out our sin.

Then Isaiah hears the voice of the Lord asking whom he shall send to his people, and Isaiah responds, "Here I am; send me!" The experience of the holy is also positively attractive. Isaiah was cleansed by God. Now, he is called by God. The experience of the holy does not end with Isaiah shaking in his boots but rather with him being raised up, and saying "Here I am Lord; send me!" And Isaiah was sent by God to proclaim relief to the poor, the widow, the orphan, and to call for justice in government and social relations. The holiness of God is the holiness of the savior. In his experience of God in the temple, Isaiah is overwhelmed by his majesty, power, and righteousness, and at the same time he is attracted to God, cleansed by God, and called to God's service: "Here I am Lord; send me!"

A God We Can See, Hear, Taste, and Touch

Our gospel lesson from today gives us another classic example of the experience of the holy, this time in Jesus Christ. It is the story of the call of Simon Peter. Simon Peter is literally minding his own business, which is fishing, when along comes Jesus. Apparently Peter has had a bad day with no fish to show for his efforts. Jesus tells him to give it one more shot, "Go out into the deep water and let down your nets." Peter whines a bit about working all night to no avail, but then agrees saying, somewhat petulantly, "If you say so, I'll let down the nets." And he does, and he catches so many fish that it almost breaks his nets, so many fish that they fill two boats, causing them to start to sink.

At this point, Peter falls down at Jesus' knees and says, "Go away from me Lord, for I am a sinful man!" Peter has encountered the holiness of the God of Israel in Jesus. In the presence of the Lord, Peter falls to the ground. He is experiencing and expressing his creatureliness. He is a man, formed of the dust, lying face down in the dust. He also experiences his sinfulness in the presence of Jesus: "Go away from me Lord, for I am a sinful man!" Like Isaiah's vision of God in the temple, Peter experiences the ethical holiness of the Lord, and he is shaken.

And like Isaiah's encounter, we know the story cannot end with Peter on his knees. The holiness of the Lord doesn't just knock us over, it also lifts us up. And sure enough, Jesus says to Peter, "Do not be afraid, from now on you will be catching people." With these words, Jesus lifts Peter up. It is a symbolic cleansing of Peter. He goes from face down in the dust to standing in the presence of the Lord.

And again, like Isaiah's vision, we know the story cannot end here. Jesus lifts Peter up not just so he can enjoy the holiness of Jesus. Jesus has holy work to do. Jesus has come to bring good news to the poor, to proclaim release to the captives and recovery of sight to the blind, to let the oppressed go free, to proclaim the year of the Lord's favor. Jesus Christ is the savior of the world, and he calls Peter to participate in that salvation. Leave your nets behind; from now on you will be fishing for people. And Peter leaves everything behind and follows Jesus. In his encounter with the holiness of

Jesus, Peter is literally overwhelmed and falls to the ground. But he is also lifted up, dusted off, and called to follow the Lord.

We are never told why Peter leaves everything behind and follows Jesus. This lack of information frustrates many people. Okay, this lack of information frustrates me! I have read too many novels where I'm made privy to every thought that goes on in the minds of characters. Unfortunately, the Gospel writers do not share this novelistic fascination with the inner working of the human psyche. Rather, what we usually get is a terse call from Jesus to follow him and an equally terse narration of disciples leaving everything behind and following. We never hear if Peter saw Jesus as a positive role model, or if Andrew admired Jesus' platform for the reform of working conditions in Galilee, or if Levi would have followed anyone to get out of the tax collecting business. It's just usually this: Jesus calls, the disciples follow. And I want to know why!

Fortunately, our gospel lesson for today does provide an answer. But it isn't found in the inner workings of the disciples' minds. It has very little to do with what Peter was thinking. Rather, it has to do with who and what he was experiencing. It was not within himself, but outside of himself, in the person of Jesus Christ, that Peter encountered the Holy One of Israel. In a flesh and blood human being, Peter is broadsided by the overwhelming power and majesty of God. The righteousness of God knocked him to the ground. In the holy presence of Jesus Christ, Peter experiences the graciousness of God that lifts him back up, looks him in the eye, and says, *follow me*. God's holiness is righteous; it is an ethical holiness, in whose presence we sense our own creatureliness and sinfulness. But God's holiness is also gracious; it lifts us up, cleanses us with holy fire, and sends us into the world in loyal service to God's salvific purposes.

There are plenty of good reasons to believe in God. As a good explanation for the existence of our finely tuned universe. As the foundation of our human moral awareness. As the basis for the hope of life after death. There are also plenty of good reasons to follow Jesus. Jesus was a charismatic Jew, a healer, a sage, a peasant revolutionary, a social prophet, to name just some of the compelling portraits of Jesus on offer these days.

But, ultimately, reasons aren't enough. We need more than reasons. We need the living God, the holy God. We need a God who doesn't just offer the best explanation for the existence of the universe but the God whose glory fills heaven and earth, whose power and majesty brings us to our knees. We need a God who is not just the foundation of our moral life but the God who is righteousness itself. We need a God who doesn't just understand our bad decisions and forgives us but the Lord who cleanses us of our sins with holy fire. We need a God who doesn't just encourage us to discover our inner directedness but the God who lifts us from the dust, stands us on our feet, and says, *come, follow me*. We need a God who doesn't wait around hoping we will discover him but, rather, the God who comes to us as a flesh and blood savior. We need a God who doesn't simply assure us that things will work out in heaven but the God who suffered and died and rose again. We need the Holy God of Israel. We need Jesus Christ. We need the fearsome love of God in flesh and bone.

SIXTH SUNDAY AFTER THE EPIPHANY, YEAR B—
1 CORINTHIANS 9:24–27

> Do you not know that in a race the runners all compete, but only one receives the prize? Run in such a way that you may win it. Athletes exercise self-control in all things; they do it to receive a perishable wreath, but we an imperishable one. So I do not run aimlessly, nor do I box as though beating the air; but I punish my body and enslave it, so that after proclaiming to others I myself should not be disqualified. (NRSV)

Slow and Steady

 Amy E. Richter

You have probably heard the old adage, *slow and steady wins the race*. That is actually not true. Fast wins the race, and I suppose steadily and consistently fast wins more often than does fast in fits and starts. I understand how the phrase works as the moral to Aesop's fable, where the swift but arrogant and lazy hare gets beat to the finish line by the plodding but unwavering tortoise. I have even taken comfort in the thought as I, slow runner that I am, keep putting one foot in front of the other, knowing that if I keep moving forward and the race course doesn't close, I will finish the race. Not win, but finish.

One of the things I have enjoyed about running marathons is that I have been able to compete in the same field, on the same course, as some of the fastest long-distance runners on the planet. When the starting gun goes off, all the runners, the speedy rabbits and the leaden turtles alike, get moving. Never mind that in a race with thousands of contestants it takes me, back in the pack with the slowpokes, a good five minutes even to cross the starting line, while the world-class runners have already passed the first-mile marker. Never mind that the winners will be finished hours, literally hours, ahead of me. This means I'm usually crossing the halfway line when the word comes through the crowd that the winner has already completed the 26.2 miles. *Wow*, I think, and with the next labored breath, *all right, only 13.1 to go.* But some days, some runs, some courses have been so beautiful that I have thought, *I wonder if the winners ever wish they were still out here running.* Sure, it must be nice to be done in just over two hours, but I'm still out here enjoying all this, and those poor winners are looking over their stats with their coaches, talking with the press about their strategies, and speculating about their next races. Me, I'm just out here in the sunshine for another couple of hours, feeling the beat of my heart, the rhythm of my breath, and trying to ignore the blister forming on my little toe. Slow and steady finishes the race, and also gets to enjoy the scenery—all of it, and in great detail—along the way. That's the prize I win when I run the race.

My favorite marathon did not attract any international superstar runners. It was a race from the town of Marathon, Wisconsin, to the town of Athens, Wisconsin. Yes, a 26.2-mile course through central Wisconsin. It was a very small field of competitors, small enough that I came in first in my division, which must have been something like "female Episcopal priests who like the color red."

A God We Can See, Hear, Taste, and Touch

What I liked most was the party at the end. Joe had gone ahead to the finish line to wait for me. He said he would be philosophizing with the locals in the agora. I was already smiling, just thinking of that. When I crossed the finish line, I was greeted by my husband, and I got a finisher's medal. The post-race party was a community potluck picnic on the lawn in the center of town. There were the usual post-marathon staples: bananas, bagels, orange slices. But someone had also made a Nesco (one of those really big crock pots people bring to church potlucks) full of chicken stew. There were bratwursts and buns, a Jell-o mold, and a tuna casserole with crunchy Chinese noodles on top. We sat on the grass in the sunshine of a perfect fall day, eating real homemade food that somebody had prepared in this little town. When they gave out the awards, people clapped, even for me, despite the fact that I turned out to be the only entrant in my category. The party at the finish line was worth the weeks of training, the long slow runs, and the blisters.

St. Paul talks about running races because he is concerned about the Christians in Corinth. Rather than being one united band of believers, what he calls elsewhere "the body of Christ," the Corinthians have divided up into little factions. They aren't shouting words of encouragement to one another as they run; they are instead arguing about who is fastest, who is strongest, whose running shoes are the prettiest, who doesn't actually belong in the race, and who doesn't actually have to run in order to get a finisher's medal. Paul is worried because many of them think that because of God's grace, they have already arrived. They believe that because they have already obtained salvation through Jesus Christ, they don't even have to enter the race. Who wants to sweat? Why risk blisters? Let's go straight to the beer truck and get the free massages in the post-race celebration tent. They thought they had their spiritual lives all sewn up, nothing more to learn or do. They were becoming self-indulgent, presuming the grace of God, and letting themselves get spiritually flabby. Their response to what God had done for them was complacency and a sense of superiority over others, rather than joyful obedience and steadfastness in practices that engender compassion, faith, hope, and charity. They were content, maybe even amused, to sit on the sidelines and throw beer bottles and banana peels onto the racecourse and laugh at the red-faced and panting runners as they went past.

St. Paul responds: Lace up your shoes, and get off the sidelines and onto the track. Put down the Ho-Hos and pick up your pace. Run, and run like you are trying to win. Run like you believe the words of the late racecar driver Dale Earnhart, "Second place is just the first place loser." Athletes are willing to exercise self-control, and they are just trying to get a perishable prize, a wreath, whose leaves will wither and die. Athletes will organize their whole lives around the single-minded pursuit of winning a race. And when they've run that race, they keep training for the next. We, Paul says, are training for a much more important prize: an imperishable prize, eternal life that will not fade, cannot be taken away, can't be wrestled away from us by the next, stronger, faster athlete who will force us to consider retirement.

Thankfully for all of us, there is enough of this imperishable prize to go around, and unlike in a race, there can be more than one winner. But you still have to run to get the prize. No one can go to the prize desk and pick it up for you. Paul doesn't even take it for granted for himself. He says, now expanding to include a boxing image as well, "So I do not run aimlessly nor do I box as though beating the air." Paul isn't just advising others from the sidelines. He knows he also must continue his purposeful training, his own pursuit of the prize. He wants the Corinthians to know that he knows what it's like, the discipline, determination, and direction demanded to win the race, to make every punch against his opponent count. He stays on course, runs the most direct route he can, makes every jab and hook connect with its target. Paul isn't a coach who goes out for a cigarette break while you're inside the gym jumping rope, doing pushups, and squeezing out one more rep. He's not eating potato chips on the sidelines while telling you to do one more lap. We can trust what he says because he's got his own regimen to follow, and he too is putting one foot in front of the other and running like his eternal life depends on it. He's in it to win it.

But he knows that his greatest opponent is neither the elite marathoner nor the top-ranked boxer. His toughest opponent is himself. So he treats himself with severity: "But I punish my body and enslave it, so that after proclaiming to others I myself shall not be disqualified." "Punish" may be an unfortunate translation. We know of so many people, especially young people, who do harmful things to their bodies, like cutting and starving. They hurt themselves physically as a way to try to gain control and manage their feelings, but this kind of self-inflicted damage doesn't result in health or victory. At best, and when noticed, it can be a cry for help, and can be treated. Paul isn't talking about that kind of self-inflicted behavior.

But he is talking about being tough on himself. The word he uses really describes something along the lines of getting a black eye. It's the same word used in the Gospel of Luke, in Jesus' story of the persistent widow and the unjust judge (Luke 18:1–8). The widow won't give up and hounds the judge, demanding that he give her justice. The judge finally relents, not because she has convinced him, or because he is ready to change his ways and do what is right, but so that "She may not wear me out by continually coming" (Luke 18:5). The "wearing out" of the judge by the widow could be translated, "giving me a black eye," "beating me black and blue." That's what Paul is describing. Coming back to the training, again and again, persisting in discipline and exercise, until he can do more than just talk about the prize, do more than just want it, but win it too. Paul wants a robust faith that shows in his life through sacrifice, obedience, persistence. He knows this is the way to win.

So, our week has started by getting ourselves to church. That's a good start. It's like showing up at the gym with our gym bag or stepping onto the trail with our running shoes on. What we do next is up to us. Will you listen to the coach, but then sit down and take a load off? Will you say, "That's interesting, coach, but I'll start next week?" Will you round up some others and go get ice cream? Or will you get to work?

Run, that you may obtain the prize. There's going to be a great party at the finish line.

Love in Flesh and Bone

SEVENTH SUNDAY AFTER THE EPIPHANY, YEAR A—MATTHEW 5:38–48

> Jesus said, "You have heard that it was said, 'An eye for an eye and a tooth for a tooth.' But I say to you, Do not resist an evildoer. But if anyone strikes you on the right cheek, turn the other also; and if anyone wants to sue you and take your coat, give your cloak as well; and if anyone forces you to go one mile, go also the second mile. Give to everyone who begs from you, and do not refuse anyone who wants to borrow from you. You have heard that it was said, 'You shall love your neighbor and hate your enemy.' But I say to you, Love your enemies and pray for those who persecute you, so that you may be children of your Father in heaven; for he makes his sun rise on the evil and on the good, and sends rain on the righteous and on the unrighteous. For if you love those who love you, what reward do you have? Do not even the tax collectors do the same? And if you greet only your brothers and sisters, what more are you doing than others? Do not even the Gentiles do the same? Be perfect, therefore, as your heavenly Father is perfect." (NRSV)

Forgive

 Joseph S. Pagano

In his short story "The Capital of the World," Ernest Hemingway begins with a joke about forgiveness. He writes, "Madrid is full of boys named Paco, which is diminutive of the name Francisco, and there is a Madrid joke about a father who came to Madrid and inserted an advertisement in the personal columns of *El Liberal* which said: PACO MEET ME AT HOTEL MONTANA NOON TUESDAY ALL IS FORGIVEN PAPA and how a squadron of Guardia Civil had to be called out to disperse the eight hundred young men who answered the advertisement."[12]

Now, on one level, this is a joke about how many boys are named Paco in Madrid. But the joke works because, at another

---

12. Hemingway, "Capital of the World," 29.

A God We Can See, Hear, Taste, and Touch

level, many people, whether they are sons or daughters, mothers or fathers, are longing for forgiveness. The offer of "all is forgiven" goes out, and hundreds of people come running. It does seem like so many of us are, in so many ways, longing for forgiveness. We may have done something or said something or didn't do something or didn't say something for which we are deeply sorry, and so we long for the cooling waters of forgiveness. Or we may have been wronged or hurt or betrayed, and we are still holding a grudge, and it is eating us up inside, and we want to just let it go, to forgive, and to get on with our lives. In so many ways, many of us are longing for the experience of true and genuine forgiveness. In so many ways, we all want to hear the message "all is forgiven."

Our parish recently surveyed people on topics they would most like to hear addressed in a sermon. Forgiveness was in the top three. People wrote in questions like: "What is forgiveness?"; "What are the steps in forgiveness?"; and "Do people need to apologize before I can forgive them?" I think these questions are reflective of our broader culture. Forgiveness is something of a hot topic these days. There is a growing body of literature on the meaning and nature of forgiveness that ranges from the scientific to self-help. At the Stanford Forgiveness Project, Frederick Luskin and his colleagues have taught hundreds of people how to forgive, and then measured its impact. They have found a general increase in health and well-being. Forgiving lowers blood pressure. It reduces the strain on the heart. It reduces depression, anger, and stress. At the International Forgiveness Institute in Madison, Wisconsin, Robert Enright and his colleagues have developed a forgiveness education curriculum for children in war-torn and impoverished areas around the globe. And, believe or not, there is a professor at Emory University, Frans de Waal, who studies forgiveness and reconciliation among monkeys and apes. This raises the obvious question: Who is better at forgiveness, monkeys or humans? Well, here's what de Waal says in his book *Peacemaking among Primates*: "Reconciliation is crucial: immediately after a fight two adversaries tend to stay away from each other, but after a time one approaches the other and tries to make friendly contact. The length of the process varies; whereas monkeys generally make up within minutes, humans can take days, years, even generations to do the same."[13] I don't know if that result is surprising or not!

Our gospel lesson for today is a classic passage about forgiveness and reconciliation. It's from the Sermon on the Mount where Jesus says, "You have heard that it was said, 'An eye for an eye and a tooth for a tooth.' But I say to you, do not resist an evildoer. But if anyone strikes you on the right cheek, turn the other also." Jesus also says, "You have heard that it was said, 'You shall love your neighbor and hate your enemy.' But I say to you, Love you enemies and pray for those who persecute you, so that you may be children of your Father in heaven; for he makes his sun rise on the evil and the good, and sends rain on the righteous and on the unrighteous." Jesus' counsel to turn the other cheek and to love our enemies has generated an enormous amount of comment and interpretation. It seems clear enough that Jesus is ruling out retaliation. He did not say, "If someone strikes on the right cheek, well then you strike him back on the right cheek." It also seems clear enough that Jesus is ruling out harboring a simmering resentment against wrongdoers. He tells us to love our enemies rather than to hate them. The critical question focuses on whether Jesus is counseling passivity in the face of evil or if he is saying something else. As surprising as it might sound, many scholars are saying that when Jesus said to turn the other cheek he was not telling us to be passive in the face of wrongdoing. Rather, they say Jesus was giving us a third alternative, beyond the typical responses of fight or flight. Turning the other cheek provides us with a way of standing up to wrongdoing and diffusing the situation without resorting to retaliation or violence. So being committed to the type of forgiveness found in turning the other cheek and loving our enemies doesn't mean being a doormat.

Here is how Walter Wink explains this passage. He begins by wondering why Jesus specifies the right cheek. He says, "How does one strike another on the right cheek, anyway? Try it. A blow by the right fist in a right-handed world would land on the left check of the opponent. To strike the right cheek with the fist would require using the left hand, but in that society the left hand was used only for

---

13. De Waal, *Peacemaking among Primates*, 2.

A God We Can See, Hear, Taste, and Touch

unclean tasks."[14] Wink continues, "The only way one could strike the right cheek with the right hand would be with the back of the right hand. What we are dealing with here is unmistakably an insult, not a fistfight. The intention is not to injure but to humiliate, to put someone in his or her place . . . a backhand slap was the normal way of admonishing inferiors."[15]

Wink claims that Jesus was addressing people who were regularly subjected to these types of indignities. They were people who were usually on the receiving end of a backhand slap. Why then, Wink asks, would Jesus tell these already humiliated people to turn the other cheek? He answers, "Because this action robs the oppressor of the power to humiliate. The person who turns the other cheek is saying, in effect, 'try again. Your first blow failed to achieve its intended effect. I deny you the power to humiliate me. I am a human being just like you. You cannot demean me.'"[16]

So turning the other cheek reasserts one's dignity in the face of an insult. But Wink says it also does more than this. Turning the other cheek also creatively disarms the other person. By turning the other cheek one deflects the person from being able to backhand you again. Now the other person, if he is to strike you again, must punch you in the nose using a fist. But that would be to treat you as an equal, and the whole point of the backhand was to demean you. According to Wink, Jesus' counsel to turn the other cheek is not telling us to become punching bags. Rather, he provides us a way to creatively, and without resort to violence, assert our humanity, refuse to succumb to humiliation, and diffuse the situation.

So when later in today's gospel lesson Jesus goes on to say to love your enemy, he was not telling us to be doormats or punching bags. Rather, he was saying, don't engage in the demeaning and dehumanizing behavior of your enemies. Despite their wrongdoing, which should not be accepted, they are human beings who deserve to be treated with dignity. And by treating them with love rather than with hatred we will be like God in heaven, who makes his sun

---

14. Wink, *Jesus and Nonviolence*, 14.
15. Ibid., 14–15.
16. Ibid., 15–16.

rise on the evil and on the good, and sends rain on the righteous and on the unrighteous.

The creative response of turning the other cheek shows how we can concretely love our enemies by diffusing the violence that would only lead to more violence, and in so doing create the context in which forgiveness and reconciliation can take place. So the upshot of this interpretation is that forgiveness is not about being a doormat or punching bag, but, rather, is about creating a way in which we can love our enemies and seek reconciliation with them.

In light of our gospel lesson today, let's return to our original question about the nature of forgiveness and how we might go about it. Jesus' counsel is clear: don't retaliate; don't hate; love your enemy. In other passages, the imperative to forgive is also clearly stated. Jesus once told Peter that he should forgive seventy times seven times! But nowhere in the Gospels does Jesus go into the details about how we are to forgive. I must confess, this lack of detail frustrates me! I want a PowerPoint presentation, with bullet points and pictures. I want to learn how to forgive in five easy steps. I want to know if by "love your enemy," Jesus means we must really "love" them, or if he means that I should just stop wishing they get run over by a bus, because that is close enough. Alas, Jesus doesn't respond to my whining, which is probably my way of trying to evade the clear meaning of Jesus' command. How, then, might I stop the whining and get on with the forgiving?

This morning I want to share a couple of recent approaches to forgiveness. One is by a psychologist and the other is by a theologian. These approaches are not exhaustive by any means. There are other extremely thoughtful and important treatments of forgiveness. My hope is that these two approaches will help us begin to flesh out how we might go about following Jesus' commandment to forgive.

The first approach comes from psychologist Robert Enright. He defines forgiveness this way: "When unjustly hurt by another, we forgive when we overcome the resentment toward the offender, not by denying our right to the resentment, but instead by trying to offer the wrongdoer compassion, benevolence, and love."[17] For

---

17. See Enright, *Forgiveness Is a Choice*, 25.

Enright, there are three important aspects of forgiveness. First, the offense is to be taken seriously. The harmful action was wrong, continues to be wrong, will always be wrong. Forgiveness does not condone or excuse wrongdoing. It doesn't say, "Oh, it was nothing" or "I know you really didn't mean it" or "Maybe I brought this upon myself." Forgiveness includes the moral claim that what was done was wrong and ought not to be repeated. Second, victims do have a moral right to anger. They were treated unjustly and a certain amount of anger is justified, because it says that what was done violated basic human dignity. When we are harmed a certain amount of resentment is morally appropriate. Third, victims choose to give up their moral right to anger and resentment. Forgiveness is a gift to the offender who does not deserve it. Forgiveness is an act of mercy.

According to Enright, people forgive for a variety of reasons. Some forgive because it is good for their psychological and physical well-being. Anger can sweep over us like a tidal wave. Anger can smolder for weeks, months, even years. Anger can raise our blood pressure and damage our hearts. Forgiveness can be a way to quiet our anger and improve our mental and physical health. Some forgive because it is good for our relationships. The anger I feel for my boss may be spilling over into how I treat my spouse and family. My anger over a bad relationship in the past may be inhibiting me from forming new, healthy relationships. Some forgive for the sake of the offender's well-being. Maybe forgiving offenders will help them to realize the error of their ways, and so help them stop their bad behavior. Maybe forgiving will allow us to improve our relation with them. And some forgive simply because they think it's the right thing to do, because God asks us to forgive regardless of how the other person responds. People forgive for a variety of reasons. The point isn't to all agree on the same reasons for forgiving. The point is to get on with the forgiving.

Enright and his colleagues have developed a process for forgiveness that includes four major phases. Forgiveness isn't as simple as flipping a switch. It takes time and reflection. The first step is uncovering our anger. This is not always an easy thing to do. We can be pretty good at pretending that nothing happened. But we need to face our feelings of anger and acknowledge the ways anger has affected our view of ourselves and our view of the world. When we are hurt we need to be honest about our suffering. Second, we need to decide to forgive. At some point, we need to recognize that the way we are dealing with our hurt is not working. We need to turn our backs on the past and look toward the future. Choosing the path of forgiveness doesn't bring immediate emotional release, but it is a necessary step on the way. The third step, then, is actually working on forgiveness. We need to work toward compassion, trying to bring the person who hurt us to mind with some sense of positive affirmation. This may be as simple as saying that we hope this person has happiness and peace. In time, we may be able to accept the pain we have suffered and ultimately to give the offender a gift that demonstrates our forgiveness. It could be as simple as sending a birthday card or as complicated as the gift of your presence at the wrongdoer's hospital bed. The final step is the release we experience from our emotional prisons. Working through the forgiveness process helps us to find meaning in the midst of suffering, helps us to discover that we are not alone, and brings us freedom to lead our lives with purpose.

Enright and his colleagues actually set up several controlled studies to test the effectiveness of the forgiveness process. They recruited people who experienced specific types of anger, and then divided them into two groups: one that received forgiveness training and another which did not. In one study, they worked with twelve women who were incest survivors. None had forgiven their abusers and all were suffering from anxiety, depression, and low self-esteem. Six were randomly selected to form a group that would be led by an educator trained in the forgiveness process to help these women work on forgiving their perpetrators. The other six received no instruction. At the end of a year, the six women in the forgiveness group improved significantly. All six were able to forgive their perpetrators. A series of psychological tests showed decreases in anxiety and depression, and increases in their sense of hopefulness for the future. The control group showed no measurable improvement. Enright claims that no other treatment program for incest survivors has produced such positive results. Forgiveness

A God We Can See, Hear, Taste, and Touch

works! You'll be happy to know that after the study concluded, the control group was offered the forgiveness training, and that they benefitted greatly from it.

Enright's approach is extremely helpful. For folks who are religious, he encourages them to draw upon their faith. However, God remains on the periphery of the discussion. Theologian Miroslav Volf brings God into the center of forgiveness. He says, "For Christians, forgiving always takes place in a triangle, involving the wrongdoer, the wronged person, and God. Take God away and the foundations of forgiveness become unsteady and may even crumble."[18] The centrality of God to forgiveness seems extremely important to me. Sinner that I am, Enright's approach can appear a bit too heroic. I so admire the strength of the people who choose to forgive, and who, with grace and compassion, work through the process of forgiveness. But speaking for myself, I know only too well the weakness of my will and the stinging wounds I carry in my heart. When I have been hurt unjustly, my blood boils and I cannot help but resent the wrongdoer. I am only too aware and ashamed of the times I thought I had forgiven someone, only to hear their name mentioned and be broadsided by a wave of anger. My heart pounds and my fists clench. But if God becomes the ground and possibility of my forgiveness, I am no longer required to perform what sometimes seems to me like an act of moral heroism. If I am to forgive because God has already forgiven me, as well as my enemy, then my forgiveness becomes a response to the free gift of God's grace. I don't have to become more than the flesh and blood, forgiven sinner that I am.

Volf, like Enright, begins by saying that forgiveness is not excusing or condoning a wrongful action. Forgiveness is, first of all, "to name the wrongdoing and to condemn it."[19] There is a moral dimension of forgiveness that points out that an injustice has occurred. Part of forgiving is saying to wrongdoers that what they have done is bad. Someone has violated the moral fabric that binds us one to another, assaulted the dignity of another human being, and that is wrong. Forgiveness says so forthrightly.

---

18. Volf, *Free of Charge*, 131.
19. Ibid., 129.

Volf, however, also notes a couple of things about wrongdoing that necessitates the move to the next phase of forgiveness. Like it or not, time doesn't run backward. Once an evil deed has been done it cannot be undone. Science fiction stories about going back in time to undo some bad deed and revising the course of our lives are, unfortunately, a matter of fantasy. Since we can't undo the past, the wrongdoing is a burden that the guilty party must bear. Without the possibility of forgiveness the burden of our wrongdoing would be intolerable.

The second element in forgiveness, then, according to Volf, is "to give wrongdoers the gift of not counting the wrongdoing against them."[20] Forgiveness is a gift. It takes a burden off the shoulders of the guilty. It is something we do for the good of another person. We, too, may benefit from the act of forgiveness. But for Volf that is not the primary thing. We don't forgive because it will help us emotionally and spiritually. Rather, forgiveness is primarily focused on the good of another. The "generous release of a genuine debt" is the heart of forgiveness.[21]

The focus on the good of the offender in forgiveness has everything to do with God. Volf says, "God is the God who forgives. We forgive because God forgives. We forgive by echoing God's forgiveness. So to understand our own forgiving we need to start with God's."[22] And for Volf, God's forgiveness begins with God's love for the world. God's love for the world does not mean God thinks everything is hunky dory. Rather, it is precisely because God loves the world and cares for the world that he condemns the wrongdoing in the world, because things aren't the way they ought to be. But rather than punish the world in strict justice, God forgives. In Scripture we hear God's forgiveness described in various ways: *God does not reckon sin; God covers our sin; God puts our wrongdoing behind God's back; God removes our transgressions as far as the east is from the west; God blots out our sin; God sweeps away our sin like the mist;* and *God doesn't even remember our sins.* God has the right

20. Ibid., 130.
21. Ibid.
22. Ibid., 131.

to condemn the wrongdoing in our world, and yet in a free gift of grace God forgives the wrongdoing of the world.

For Volf, the way God forgives the sins of the world is through the life, death, and resurrection of Jesus Christ. God doesn't just condemn the sin of the world but, also, through the incarnation of Jesus, bears its burden in God's very self. Through a blessed exchange in the union of God and humanity in the person of Christ, God takes our sins upon himself and extinguishes them, and so Christ's righteousness becomes our righteousness. The forgiveness that we are to pass on to others is the forgiveness we have in union with Christ. Not because we are moral heroes or because we seek our own well-being, but because we are forgiven sinners.

When Volf says that our forgiving should echo the forgiveness of God, it sounds pretty similar to Jesus' statement in our gospel lesson: "Love your enemies and pray for those who persecute you, so that you may be children of your Father in heaven; for he makes his sun rise on the evil and on the good, and sends rain on the righteous and on the unrighteous." God is the God who forgives. We forgive because God forgives. We forgive by echoing God's forgiveness. As Walter Wink puts it, "In the final analysis, then, love of enemies is trusting God for the miracle of divine forgiveness. If God can forgive, redeem, and transform me, I must also believe that God can work such wonders with anyone. Love of enemies is seeing one's oppressors through the prism of the Reign of God—not only as they now are but also as they can become: transformed by the power of God."[23]

It does seem like so many of us are longing for forgiveness these days. We want to hear a message that says, "All is forgiven." We want to put away our past mistakes and failings, and we want to let go of our grudges and anger. We want to move into a new future without fear and where our souls are free.

In our gospel lesson for today we hear Jesus tell us to turn the other cheek and to love our enemies. As we have seen, in this passage Jesus was not asking us to become doormats or punching bags. Rather, he was saying that there is a better way than the way of anger

---

23. Wink, *Jesus and Nonviolence*, 68–69.

and vengeance. He calls us to find creative ways to resist wrongdoing, to affirm our dignity in the face of assault, and to affirm the humanity of the wrongdoer at the same time. By loving and forgiving our enemies we participate in the miracle of divine forgiveness. But it is not easy, and Jesus provides no detailed explanation of how we should go about it. Some may find Enright's approach a helpful way to flesh out what the process of forgiveness should look like. Others may find Volf's approach helpful. The point is not to just think about forgiveness but to start doing it. Maybe Jesus was wise not to give us a theory or a step-by-step process for forgiveness. Maybe he was wise simply to command us to forgive. Just start doing it. Happily, haltingly, or somewhere in between, start forgiving. If something helps us to forgive, then thanks be to God! If we mess up in our attempts to forgive, then I expect God's forgiveness on the cross of Christ covers those failures as well. Ask for forgiveness and try again. And pray, as Jesus taught us, *forgive us our trespasses as we forgive those who trespass against us.*

Eighth Sunday after the Epiphany, Year C—
1 Corinthians 15:51–58

> Listen, I will tell you a mystery! We will not all die, but we will all be changed, in a moment, in the twinkling of an eye, at the last trumpet. For the trumpet will sound, and the dead will be raised imperishable, and we will be changed. For this perishable body must put on imperishability, and this mortal body must put on immortality. When this perishable body puts on imperishability, and this mortal body puts on immortality, then the saying that is written will be fulfilled: "Death has been swallowed up in victory." "Where, O death, is your victory? Where, O death, is your sting?" The sting of death is sin, and the power of sin is the law. But thanks be to God, who gives us the victory through our Lord Jesus Christ. Therefore, my beloved, be steadfast, immovable, always excelling in the work of the Lord, because you know that in the Lord your labor is not in vain. (NRSV)

A God We Can See, Hear, Taste, and Touch

Resurrection Bodies

 Joseph S. Pagano

There are some days, when the conditions are just right, that I ache literally from head to toe. In my left foot, between my third and fourth toes, I have a neuroma that formed after nerve damage. It feels like a small pebble imbedded in the ball of my foot. One misstep and the nerves fire, causing my toes to sting and burn. I've had three knee surgeries, one on my left to repair a torn anterior cruciate ligament, and two on my right to repair a torn meniscus. There is a spot on the inside of my right knee that if banged on the edge of a coffee table will cause me to collapse in a heap of pain. I have a herniated disk in my lower back that is sore to the touch, and on a bad day pain radiates down through my backside and along the back of my legs. I have a torn right rotator cuff that wakes me in the middle of the night if I sleep in an awkward position. The top of my head doesn't ache so much as it feels funny, as my increasingly bald head reveals the scars from old head cuts that had to be stitched up in emergency rooms. If the barometric pressure drops, if I sleep on my wrong side, if I reach for something behind me without turning my body, I can ache for days.

And yet, as strange as it may sound, I have a certain fondness for these aches and pains. They remind me of experiences I cherish, experiences that have made me the person that I am today. The nerve damage in my foot reminds me of a trip to northern California, hiking in a hushed cathedral grove of giant sequoias, 250 feet high and 30 feet around, and the errant step while carrying a heavy pack that caused the injury. My sore knees remind me of the years I spent playing soccer, the exhilaration of play in the crisp autumn air, my thighs burning from exertion, the almost perfect transfer of energy in a well-struck ball, the compression, release, low trajectory, and ropey sound as the ball hit the back of the net. My sore lower back reminds me of the heavy packs I have carried up and flopped down on mountain tops. Nothing can ever taste as

109

good as a salami and cheese sandwich, leaning back on my pack, looking at the distant peaks. My sore right shoulder reminds me of years of throwing baseballs. I choose not to recall the thousands of wild throws that flew into backstops or fizzled in the dirt. Rather, I remember cutting off the throw from left field, turning and throwing a perfect strike to my catcher, beating the runner to home plate by two steps. The funny scars on the top of my head remind me of sledding trips in the Pocono Mountains with my dad and brothers, racing down the hills on our Flexi Fliers, pretending we were on the Olympic luge team, until I hit my head on a trailer hitch. Some mornings, when I shake out a few ibuprofen pills and wash them down with a cup of black coffee, I thank God for my aching body that has allowed me to experience so much joy and pain.

I recognize, however, that not everybody will or should feel the same way about all their bodily pains. Speaking for myself, I hate cancer. I hate cancer for the enormous pain it caused my mother-in-law and father-in-law. I hate cancer because it killed them way too young. I hate cancer because my wife still cries because she misses her parents so much. I hate cancer for what it has done to people I love. I hate cancer for what it does to people I don't know. Intellectually, I know—because I have read up on the problem of suffering and evil—that genetic mutation, which is the engine that has driven the amazing development of life in the universe, is also the same process that produces cancer. If the DNA in germ cells is able to mutate and produce new forms of life, the DNA of somatic cells must also be able to mutate and produce cancer. I know you can't have one without the other. There is an inevitable shadow side to the evolutionary process. It will yield not only great fruitfulness, but it will also produce ragged edges and blind alleys. I get it. But I still hate cancer.

We may experience our body as a friend or as an enemy. Sometimes, maybe while running, eating, playing, loving—when energy, vigor, and endorphins are flowing—we may feel our bodies to be so much a part of ourselves, that we are our bodies. Other times, maybe when illness strikes, when hunger gnaws, when muscles tear, when bones snap, we may feel betrayed by our bodies, that our bodies are separate from our selves. This tension has led some

A God We Can See, Hear, Taste, and Touch

to say that our bodies and souls are separate. If so, then the body is a temporary container or a prison cell in which my true self, my soul is trapped. Someday, maybe after death, my soul will escape this bodily prison and be free to return to its heavenly home. The body will decay and deteriorate, while my soul will find itself in the heavenly realm of invisible, immortal, wise souls. In the meantime, the body is a temporary, inessential part of my identity. Best not get too attached to it.

In our epistle lesson for today, Paul is dealing with some folks within the Corinthian community who thought in terms of a separation between body and spirit. Paul had gotten word that some were saying that there was no resurrection of the dead. It's not that they were denying the afterlife—they probably thought that the spirit survived after death. It's just that they didn't think the afterlife would be gained through an act of new creation by God in the resurrection of the dead. The spirit would live on after the body died and moldered in the grave. Earlier in the letter, we got hints that these folks—perhaps an upper-class elite—thought in terms of the independence and superiority of the spirit. In bizarre attempts to demonstrate the freedom of the spirit from the body, some were engaged in licentious behavior, while others were engaged in asceticism. They were flip sides of the same coin. The spirit is separate, free, superior to the body. Life after death will not include the body. Good riddance! Life after death does not occur through resurrection but, rather, through the continued life of the spirit that will escape the prison of the body.

Paul is not amused. For Paul the truth of the gospel rests upon the truth of Jesus having been raised from the dead. If that claim were false, then Paul's work has been an exercise in futility. If the message that Paul received and passed on—that Christ died in accordance with the Scriptures and was buried and raised on the third day—were false, then every Christian's faith would be in vain. The promise of salvation would be worthless and void. Everyone would remain captive to sin. The dead, who were baptized and faithful to Christ, will have gone to a dismal place of no return. The yearning of Israel for the transformation of the ages would be pointless. The principalities and powers and bullies of this age would still reign. Our last enemy, death, would still get the last laugh.

"But, in fact," Paul says, "Christ has been raised from the dead, the first fruits of those who have died" (1 Cor 15:20). As a Jew, Paul did not see a strict separation between body and spirit or body and soul. In the Old Testament, we *are* our bodies, as we *are* our souls. Human life is bodily life. The idea of life without a body, in this life or the next, makes no sense. As a Pharisaic Jew, Paul held that the resurrection of the dead is God's ultimate act of salvation. In the world to come, God's people would be redeemed, nature would be recreated, and God's faithful would be rescued from death. This rescue meant resurrection. Life in the world to come, if it were to be in any recognizable sense human life, would be bodily life. As a Pharisaic Jew who believed Jesus to be the Messiah, Paul saw God's raising Jesus Christ from the dead as the inauguration of God's salvation. Jesus Christ is the first fruits of those who have died, which means he is an anticipatory promise of the general resurrection to come. In the resurrection of Jesus Christ, the last act in the drama of salvation has begun.

The question for Paul then isn't whether we will be bodily resurrected or not but rather what the resurrection body will be like. Paul says, "In the twinkling of an eye, at the last trumpet . . . the dead will be raised imperishable, and we will be changed. For this perishable body must put on imperishability, and this mortal body must put on immortality" (15:52–53). At the resurrection, through an act of God, we will be raised with bodies that will be fit for life in the age to come. Earlier, Paul had used the image of the seed and the plant. God gives the seed a body fit for its life as a seed, and when it is sown and dies, God gives the plant that rises a body that is fit for its life as a plant. Like the seed, we have been given a natural body that is fit for life in this world, and like the plant, we will be given a body in the resurrection that will be fit for life in the world to come. The "spiritual body" that Paul speaks of in verse 44 is therefore best thought of as body that will appropriate to life in the new age under the Spirit. *This perishable body must put on imperishability, and this mortal body must put on immortality.*

Our resurrected bodies will therefore be both different and the same as our earthly bodies. They will be different because the perishable parts, the parts of our bodies that are suited to this life but not to life in the world to come, will not be raised. As Paul says, "flesh and blood cannot inherit the kingdom of God" (15:50). But, as the image of the seed and the plant suggests, our resurrected bodies will also be the same as our earthly bodies as God in the act of resurrection will change our mortal bodies into spiritual bodies. This is not the transmigration of our souls, but rather the resurrection of our bodies.

For Paul, our resurrection bodies will be similar to Jesus' body after his resurrection. Paul says, "just as we have borne the image of the man of dust, we will also bear the image of the man from heaven" (15:49). Our earthly lineage goes back to Adam. Our heavenly lineage goes back to Christ, and with his resurrection our own destinies have been sealed. In Jesus' death and resurrection, death has been defeated, swallowed up in God's victory. By virtue of our baptisms, in which we are buried with Christ in his death and by which we share in his resurrection, Christians can now shout at and even taunt death in gratitude to the God who has saved us: "Where, O death, is your victory? Where, O death is your sting?" (15:55).

And this is good news! This is good news because we are promised that beyond the grave we have a place in the world to come when God will put everything to rights, when God will wipe away every tear, when death and crying and mourning and pain will be no more. This is good news because the bodies that have enabled us to experience so much joy and so much pain will be transformed. The parts of our bodies that hurt and gnaw and wound and die will be no more. The parts of our bodies that have loved our spouses, held our children, hugged our friends, climbed mountains, thrown baseballs, run marathons, delighted in sunsets, danced the Cha-Cha, sung the doxology, knelt in prayer; the bodies that have made us who we are, the bodies that we are, will be redeemed, transformed into bodies fit for life in the age to come. Our bodies—made one with Christ's body, who ate and drank, slept and awoke, hungered and wept, died and rose again—honored in

Love in Flesh and Bone

their goodness, redeemed in their vulnerability, resurrected in the kingdom of God.

LAST SUNDAY AFTER THE EPIPHANY, YEAR A—
MATTHEW 17:1–9

> Six days later, Jesus took with him Peter and James and his brother John and led them up a high mountain, by themselves. And he was transfigured before them, and his face shone like the sun, and his clothes became dazzling white. Suddenly there appeared to them Moses and Elijah, talking with him. Then Peter said to Jesus, "Lord, it is good for us to be here; if you wish, I will make three dwellings here, one for you, one for Moses, and one for Elijah." While he was still speaking, suddenly a bright cloud overshadowed them, and from the cloud a voice said, "This is my Son, the Beloved; with him I am well pleased; listen to him!" When the disciples heard this, they fell to the ground and were overcome by fear. But Jesus came and touched them, saying, "Get up and do not be afraid." And when they looked up, they saw no one except Jesus himself alone. As they were coming down the mountain, Jesus ordered them, "Tell no one about the vision until after the Son of Man has been raised from the dead." (NRSV)

Seeing Jesus

 Joseph S. Pagano

On a recent trip, hiking in the Dolomites in Northern Italy, I saw Jesus.

Amy and I were hiking one of the most spectacular mountain routes in this portion of the Alps. It is a type of hike that I love, moving through forest, hugging mountain streams, and then breaking through the tree line along an exposed ridge that is surrounded by snow covered peaks. The air was crisp and clear, the sky blue except for a few high-flying clouds, the jagged mountains in Austria visible on the horizon.

A God We Can See, Hear, Taste, and Touch

As we neared the peak, I grew more and more eager to reach the summit. I think it must be just over the next rise. It never is. It always turns out to involve a few more climbs and probably some scrambling at the top. I make this mistake all the time, because I'm usually tired at this point, maybe a bit dehydrated, ready to ditch my pack. I want to sit down, untie the laces on my boots, drink some hot tea, and eat peanut butter sandwiches. Above all, I want to enjoy the push of the wind, the taste of the glacial air, and the panoramic views.

We walked along the exposed side of the ridge and then bore right toward the summit. As we began a bit of a corkscrew to the summit, I saw Jesus, arms stretched out across the blue sky. I must admit, my heart jumped a little at first. I'm not as young as I used to be. Maybe I was suffering from a little altitude sickness. Had I lost my footing and fell? Is this how it ends, a small hiccup in consciousness, and then into the arms of the Lord? Was this quite literally the end of the line for me?

Turns out, it was a larger-than-life, wooden crucifix. The wood of the cross and the corpus had been bleached a grayish white by the elements. Jesus' body was terribly contorted. His head was turned down and to the right, slumped below his shoulders and arms. His face was full of pain and sorrow. His right leg was bent and angled across his torso, creating an inverted S-curve with his body. Muscles strained and tendons stretched on his crucified arms and shoulders, his rib cage protruded from his side, and his fingers splayed from the nails in his palms.

Slipping off my pack, I looked up at Jesus on the cross—blue skies above, snow capped mountains in the distance, field and forest below—and I contemplated the juxtaposition of the mysteries of creation and cross. Jesus Christ "is the image of the invisible God, the firstborn of all creation; for in him all things in heaven and on earth were created" (Col 1:15-16). And Jesus Christ is also the one through whom all things were wonderfully recreated, because through him "God was pleased to reconcile to himself all things, whether on earth or in heaven, by making peace through the blood of his cross" (Col 1:20). Creation. Cross. Reconciliation. I sensed their deep connection in Jesus, but I really couldn't make sense of how they all fit together. I was befuddled, but grateful to have met Jesus on the mountaintop. My heart told me something important was being said there, but my mind couldn't grasp it.

I learned later that the Dolomites are filled with images of Christ. Many peaks there have crosses or crucifixes at the top. A few trails we hiked had stations of the cross along the way. There is even a Santa Croce Church, elevation 2045 meters, located at the foot of Mount Santa Croce, accessible by cable car if you don't want to make the hike.

I understand this desire to create a sanctuary on top of a mountain. It's exhilarating to be on a mountain peak. All the pain and the sweat of the climb seems worth it when you finally reach the top of the mountain, and, there, turning in whatever direction you may, you can see for miles and miles. You can see the valleys and the forests spreading out below you, and off in the distance you can see mountain ranges that are no higher than you are at that moment. It is so stunning, so beautiful, that you want to prolong or capture the moment. When I first make it onto the summit of a mountain and finally throw off my pack, I feel like I never want to go back down again. I always think about how amazing it would be to set up camp right there on the top, sleeping under stars.

But as the day wears on, mountaintops become very cold, very quickly. And you really don't want to be sleeping on the peak where you are exposed to the elements of rain and wind and lightning. It always amazes me how quickly I can go from overheated on the way up to shivering in freezing sweat when I'm on the top. I often lug a camera along on a hike so that I can try to capture the breathtaking views from a peak. But the pictures never offer more than a thin reminder of the original experience. As much as you may want to capture or prolong the moment you cannot. Mountaintop experiences are wonderful and awesome, but they are short lived. At some point, you have to go back down.

It's no wonder that mountaintops are key symbols for intense religious experiences. Think of Mount Olympus as the home of the Greek gods. Think of Mount Fuji, revered by many Japanese Buddhists as sacred. Think of Mount Sinai where Moses encounters Yahweh. The mountaintop, as the place where heaven and earth

A God We Can See, Hear, Taste, and Touch

meet, becomes a symbol for the encounter between God and human beings. Perhaps that's why people refer to moments of great clarity or insight as "peak experiences." In these moments, these peak experiences, it seems like the veil that covers reality is peeled back for a moment, and there we catch a glimpse of the splendor and glory of God. Somehow all of creation seems infused with light and power.

Perhaps you have experienced something like this in your own lives. For some, this may be the experience of having your breath taken away as you walked out under a clear night sky, the starry heavens seeming to glow with a billion pinpoints of light. Or perhaps you experienced this when you got up early in the morning and stood transfixed by the brilliant burst of light at sunrise. For some, it may have been in a private moment of prayer, when you felt the overwhelming presence of God's Spirit in a real and tangible way. Or maybe you felt the presence of God at an evening worship service when the candlelit church somehow radiated with the glow of God's incarnate love. In these moments, we may feel an exhilaration similar to what we feel when we reach the mountaintop. These are moments of great insight and clarity, and we wish we could somehow prolong or capture them. But like those real mountaintop experiences, these peak experiences don't last. At some point, you have to go back down.

In our gospel lesson for today, we hear of one of the great mountaintop experiences of all time. Jesus leads the disciples Peter, James, and John up a high mountain to pray. This may not have seemed like a big deal to the disciples at first. Jesus would often take some time away from the crowds for prayer, especially when things got a bit crazy. But on this day, all of a sudden, the heavens were torn open. There, on the high mountaintop, Jesus was transfigured, and the disciples got a glimpse into the true nature of Jesus. They see him transfused with light, the brightness of God's glory shining through him. For a moment, all of their senses become fully alive, their vision sharpens, and they see through the veil of the everyday into the divine reality—and they are dazzled. They see Jesus as he truly is—God's beloved Son. And with him, they also see two of the great figures of the Old Testament, Moses and Elijah. I don't think it's a coincidence that it is Moses and Elijah who are with Jesus on the mountaintop. They both had their own mountaintop experiences. In the Old Testament story, we learned of Moses who went up to the top of Mount Sinai to receive the commandments, and where he encountered the glory of the Lord. Elijah had his own mountaintop experience at Mount Horeb, where God comes to him not in the thunder or wind, but in a still, small voice. So there is Jesus, standing on the mountaintop, bathed in God's glory, with Moses and Elijah standing beside him. The disciples must have thought they hit the holy trifecta of mountaintop experiences.

Peter's response to all this is quite natural. It's also not quite right. I think that is why I love Peter so much. He is always responding in a very human, very natural way. And he is nearly always getting it wrong. Not because he isn't trying, but because he is human. Peter sees Jesus transfigured before him, and he says, "Lord, it is good that we are here. If you wish, I will make three tents here, one for you, one for Moses, and one for Elijah" (Matt 17:4). Peter, like many of us, wants to somehow capture or prolong the moment. If he can just put up some tents, maybe construct some type of monument, maybe even a sanctuary, then somehow, someway he might be able to preserve the experience of God's glory. Peter, like many of us, wants to stay on the mountaintop as long as he can.

But he could not. As much as he wanted to capture that moment, Peter eventually had to go back down the mountain. When God's voice speaks from the cloud, it does not say, "This is my Son, the Beloved, build a dwelling for him on the mountaintop away from all the troubles and pain of the world." No, the voice of God says, "This is my Son, the Beloved; with him I am well pleased; listen to him." Listen to him, and follow him. And they did. Jesus went back down from the mountain and the disciples followed him.

What Peter failed to understand was that God had work for Jesus to do back down in the valley. Jesus came to meet people not just in "peak experiences," but also in the pain and toil and humdrum of everyday life. From this point on in the gospel, everything will move toward Jerusalem, toward Jesus' suffering and death and resurrection. And it will not be an easy way. It will be the way of

A God We Can See, Hear, Taste, and Touch

costly service. And Jesus calls his disciples down from the mountaintop to follow him in this way of costly service.

Mountaintop experiences are wonderful. They are special moments when we feel or see the presence of God with great clarity or heightened insight, peak experiences when we feel that the heavens have been torn open and we see the divine glory for what it truly is. But we cannot live on the mountaintop. Try as we may to prolong or capture the moment, we eventually have to go back down, down to the seemingly less extraordinary moments in our lives. But that is what we are called to do. To live out our lives in the flat places, the rough terrains, and the valleys of everyday life.

In the film *Shadowlands*, C. S. Lewis has found out that his wife, Joy, is dying. As a boy, Lewis had seen a part of England called the Golden Valley, and he thought it was heaven. So he and Joy go looking for it. When they find it, they have their own mountaintop experience while looking down at the beautiful view of the English countryside. Lewis tells his wife, "I'm not waiting for anything new to happen. I'm here now; that's enough." His wife replies, "It's not going to last, Jack." Lewis doesn't want to talk about that. He says, "Let's not spoil the moment." But Joy responds, "It doesn't spoil it. It makes it real. I'm going to die. And the pain is part of the happiness now. That's the deal."

That's the deal. Our lives include peaks and valleys, joy and sorrow, life and death. Jesus leads us up the mountain to see the glory of the Lord, and Jesus leads us back down the mountain in the way of costly service. As much as we may want to, we cannot live on the mountaintop. Eventually, we have to go back down. I think this is why every year, on the last Sunday before Lent begins, we read the story of Jesus' transfiguration. For many, Lent is a special season of penitence and fasting. It is a time when we examine our lives and try to turn away from those things that separate us from the love of God. This time of self-examination and repentance can seem more like passing through a valley than sitting on a mountaintop. But as we prepare to move through this valley, the transfiguration of Jesus reminds us that we are following none other than God's beloved Son. This is the Jesus who, on the way down from the mountain, promised his disciples that they would see him risen from the dead at the far end of their journey. This is the same Jesus who invites us into the keeping of a holy Lent as we prepare ourselves to experience once again the good news of his glorious resurrection at Easter. This is the same Christ who promises us that we, too, will see the risen Lord at the far end of our earthly journey.

In the high peaks of the Dolomites, at the foot of the cross, I finish eating my peanut butter sandwiches. It's getting cold now. I repack my gear and I look up at the cross once more. I am grateful for an image of the crucified Jesus rather than a transfigured Lord on the mountain top. If it were an image of the transfiguration, it would have seemed wrong. When Peter wanted to construct a sanctuary for the resplendent Lord on the mountaintop, Jesus said *no*. He had to go to Jerusalem, be handed over to suffering and death, and to rise again on the third day. Somehow, an image of Jesus on the cross makes more sense here. I look into the face of the Lord and say a silent prayer thanking him for the beauty of sky and mountains and snow, for muscles that ache with exhaustion, for a heart than thumps with exertion, for eyes that fill with light, and for skin that prickles in the wind. I give thanks for the refreshment of vacation and for a vocation I love. I ask Jesus to keep my wife safe on the descent and to keep watch over all those who hike on the mountain this day. I loop the straps of my pack over my shoulders, fasten and tighten the straps, and head back down the mountain.

Bibliography

Augustine of Hippo. *Confessions*. New York: Penguin Classics, 1961.
The Book of Common Prayer (1928). New York: The Church Pension Fund, 1928.
The Book of Common Prayer (1979). New York: Seabury, 1979.
Breidenthal, Thomas E. *Christian Households: The Sanctification of Nearness*. Cambridge, MA: Cowley, 1997.
De Waal, Frans. *Peacemaking among Primates*. Cambridge, MA: Harvard University Press, 1990.
Eagleton, Terry. *How to Read Literature*. New Haven, CT: Yale University Press, 2013.
Enright, Robert. *Forgiveness Is a Choice*. Washington, DC: American Psychological Association, 2001.
Fillon, Mike. "The Real Face of Jesus: Advances in forensic science reveal the most famous face in history." No pages. Online: http://www.popularmechanics.com/science/health/forensics/1282186.
Greene, Graham. *The Heart of the Matter*. London: Penguin, 1971.
Hemingway, Ernest. "The Capital of the World." In *The Complete Short Stories of Ernest Hemingway*. New York: Charles Scribner's Sons, 1987.
Hull, John M. *Hellenistic Magic and the Synoptic Tradition*. Studies in Biblical Theology. Second Series 28. Naperville, IL: Allenson, 1974.
Jeffers, Ann. *Magic and Divination in Ancient Palestine and Syria*. Studies in the History and Culture of the Ancient Near East 8. Edited by B. Halpern and M. H. E. Weippert. Leiden, NL: Brill, 1996.

Bibliography

L'Engle, Madeleine. *Penguins and Golden Calves.* Wheaton, IL: Harold Shaw, 1996.

Luz, Ulrich. *Matthew 1–7: A Commentary.* Edited by Helmut Koester. Translated by James E. Crouch. Hermeneia. Minneapolis, MN: Fortress, 2007.

Morgan, Robert. *Come Let Us Adore Him: Stories Behind the Most Cherished Christmas Hymns.* Nashville, TN: J. Countryman, 2005.

Otto, Rudolf. *The Idea of the Holy.* New York: Oxford University Press, 1958.

Plantinga, Cornelius Jr. *Not the Way It's Supposed to Be: A Breviary of Sin.* Grand Rapids, MI: William B. Eerdmans, 1995.

Richter, Amy E. *Enoch and the Gospel of Matthew.* Princeton Theological Monograph Series. Eugene, OR: Pickwick, 2012.

———. "Heavenly Body: A Female Priest Gives a New Definition to 'Sunday Best.'" *New York Times Magazine,* April 22, 2012.

———. "The Ripped, Bikini-Clad Reverend." No pages. Online: http://www.nytimes.com/2012/04/22/magazine/the-ripped-bikini-clad-reverend.html?_r=0.

Robb-Dover, Kristina. "Women Body Builders: Why the Church Needs More of Them." No pages. Online: http://blog.beliefnet.com/fellowshipofsaintsandsinners/2012/04/women-body-builders-why-the-church-needs-more-of-them.html.

Volf, Miroslav. *Free of Charge: Giving and Forgiving in a Culture Stripped of Grace.* Grand Rapids, MI: Zondervan, 2005.

Wink, Walter. *Jesus and Nonviolence: A Third Way.* Minneapolis, MN: Fortress, 2003.

Wordsworth, William. "Lines Composed a Few Miles above Tintern Abbey, on Revisiting the Banks of the Wye during a Tour. July 13, 1798." In *The Penguin Book of English Verse.* Edited by John Hayward. Harmondsworth, UK: Penguin, 1956.

www.ingramcontent.com/pod-product-compliance
Lightning Source LLC
Chambersburg PA
CBHW071623170426
43195CB00038B/2042